# HOPE HAS COME

*The Promise of Christ in All of Scripture*

THE DAILY GRACE CO.

# STUDY SUGGESTIONS

*We believe that the Bible is true, trustworthy, and timeless and that it is vitally important for all believers. These study suggestions are intended to help you more effectively study Scripture as you seek to know and love God through His Word.*

## SUGGESTED STUDY TOOLS

- A Bible

- A double-spaced, printed copy of the Scripture passages that this study covers. You can use a website like *www.biblegateway.com* to copy the text of a passage and print out a double-spaced copy to be able to mark on easily

- A journal to write notes or prayers

- Pens, colored pencils, and highlighters

- A dictionary to look up unfamiliar words

## HOW TO USE THIS STUDY

Begin your study time in prayer. Ask God to reveal Himself to you, to help you understand what you are reading, and to transform you with His Word (Psalm 119:18).

Before you read what is written in each day of the study itself, read the assigned passages of Scripture for that day. Use your double-spaced copy to circle, underline, highlight, draw arrows, and mark in any way you would like to help you dig deeper as you work through a passage.

Read the daily written content provided for the current study day.

Answer the questions that appear at the end of each study day.

# HOW TO STUDY THE BIBLE

The inductive method provides tools for deeper and more intentional Bible study. To study the Bible inductively, work through the steps below after reading background information on the book.

### 1. OBSERVATION & COMPREHENSION
Key question: What does the text say?

After reading the daily Scripture in its entirety at least once, begin working with smaller portions of the Scripture. Read a passage of Scripture repetitively, and then mark the following items in the text:

- Key or repeated words and ideas
- Key themes
- Transition words (Ex: therefore, but, because, if/then, likewise, etc.)
- Lists
- Comparisons and contrasts
- Commands
- Unfamiliar words (look these up in a dictionary)
- Questions you have about the text

### 2. INTERPRETATION
Key question: What does the text mean?

Once you have annotated the text, work through the following steps to help you interpret its meaning:

- Read the passage in other versions for a better understanding of the text.
- Read cross-references to help interpret Scripture with Scripture.
- Paraphrase or summarize the passage to check for understanding.
- Identify how the text reflects the metanarrative of Scripture, which is the story of creation, fall, redemption, and restoration.
- Read trustworthy commentaries if you need further insight into the meaning of the passage.

## 3 APPLICATION
### Key Question: How should the truth of this passage change me?

Bible study is not merely an intellectual pursuit. The truths about God, ourselves, and the gospel that we discover in Scripture should produce transformation in our hearts and lives. Answer the following questions as you consider what you have learned in your study:

- What attributes of God's character are revealed in the passage?

    Consider places where the text directly states the character of God, as well as how His character is revealed through His words and actions.

- What do I learn about myself in light of who God is?

    Consider how you fall short of God's character, how the text reveals your sin nature, and what it says about your new identity in Christ.

- How should this truth change me?

    A passage of Scripture may contain direct commands telling us what to do or warnings about sins to avoid in order to help us grow in holiness. Other times our application flows out of seeing ourselves in light of God's character. As we pray and reflect on how God is calling us to change in light of His Word, we should be asking questions like, "How should I pray for God to change my heart?" and "What practical steps can I take toward cultivating habits of holiness?"

# THE ATTRIBUTES OF GOD

### ETERNAL

God has no beginning and no end. He always was, always is, and always will be.

HAB. 1:12 / REV. 1:8 / IS. 41:4

### FAITHFUL

God is incapable of anything but fidelity. He is loyally devoted to His plan and purpose.

2 TIM. 2:13 / DEUT. 7:9
HEB. 10:23

### GOOD

God is pure; there is no defilement in Him. He is unable to sin, and all He does is good.

GEN. 1:31 / PS. 34:8 / PS. 107:1

### GRACIOUS

God is kind, giving us gifts and benefits we do not deserve.

2 KINGS 13:23 / PS. 145:8
IS. 30:18

### HOLY

God is undefiled and unable to be in the presence of defilement. He is sacred and set-apart.

REV. 4:8 / LEV. 19:2 / HAB. 1:13

### INCOMPREHENSIBLE & TRANSCENDENT

God is high above and beyond human understanding. He is unable to be fully known.

PS. 145:3 / IS. 55:8-9
ROM. 11:33-36

### IMMUTABLE

God does not change. He is the same yesterday, today, and tomorrow.

1 SAM. 15:29 / ROM. 11:29
JAMES 1:17

### INFINITE

God is limitless. He exhibits all of His attributes perfectly and boundlessly.

ROM. 11:33-36 / IS. 40:28
PS. 147:5

### JEALOUS

God is desirous of receiving the praise and affection He rightly deserves.

EX. 20:5 / DEUT. 4:23-24
JOSH. 24:19

### JUST

God governs in perfect justice. He acts in accordance with justice. In Him, there is no wrongdoing or dishonesty.

IS. 61:8 / DEUT. 32:4 / PS. 146:7-9

### LOVING

God is eternally, enduringly, steadfastly loving and affectionate. He does not forsake or betray His covenant love.

JN. 3:16 / EPH. 2:4-5 / 1 JN. 4:16

## MERCIFUL
God is compassionate, withholding from us the wrath that we deserve.

TITUS 3:5 / PS. 25:10
LAM. 3:22-23

## OMNIPOTENT
God is all-powerful; His strength is unlimited.

MAT. 19:26 / JOB 42:1-2
JER. 32:27

## OMNIPRESENT
God is everywhere; His presence is near and permeating.

PROV. 15:3 / PS. 139:7-10
JER. 23:23-24

## OMNISCIENT
God is all-knowing; there is nothing unknown to Him.

PS. 147:4 / I JN. 3:20
HEB. 4:13

## PATIENT
God is long-suffering and enduring. He gives ample opportunity for people to turn toward Him.

ROM. 2:4 / 2 PET. 3:9 / PS. 86:15

## SELF-EXISTENT
God was not created but exists by His power alone.

PS. 90:1-2 / JN. 1:4 / JN. 5:26

## SELF-SUFFICIENT
God has no needs and depends on nothing, but everything depends on God.

IS. 40:28-31 / ACTS 17:24-25
PHIL. 4:19

## SOVEREIGN
God governs over all things; He is in complete control.

COL. 1:17 / PS. 24:1-2
1 CHRON. 29:11-12

## TRUTHFUL
God is our measurement of what is fact. By Him we are able to discern true and false.

JN. 3:33 / ROM. 1:25 / JN. 14:6

## WISE
God is infinitely knowledgeable and is judicious with His knowledge.

IS. 46:9-10 / IS. 55:9 / PROV. 3:19

## WRATHFUL
God stands in opposition to all that is evil. He enacts judgment according to His holiness, righteousness, and justice.

PS. 69:24 / JN. 3:36 / ROM. 1:18

# METANARRATIVE OF SCRIPTURE

## Creation

In the beginning, God created the universe. He made the world and everything in it. He created humans in His own image to be His representatives on the earth.

## Fall

The first humans, Adam and Eve, disobeyed God by eating from the fruit of the Tree of Knowledge of Good and Evil. Their disobedience impacted the whole world. The punishment for sin is death, and because of Adam's original sin, all humans are sinful and condemned to death.

## Redemption

God sent His Son to become a human and redeem His people. Jesus Christ lived a sinless life but died on the cross to pay the penalty for sin. He resurrected from the dead and ascended into heaven. All who put their faith in Jesus are saved from death and freely receive the gift of eternal life.

## Restoration

One day, Jesus Christ will return again and restore all that sin destroyed. He will usher in a new heaven and new earth where all who trust in Him will live eternally with glorified bodies in the presence of God.

"WE AWAIT HIS SECOND COMING WHEN HE WILL LIGHT THE WORLD WITH HIS GLORY."

*The Advent
Candle Lighting Tradition* 13

## WEEK ONE
## HOPE

DAY 1   15
*Candle Lighting Day
Scripture Memory*

DAY 2   19
*The Hope of the World*

DAY 3   23
*Hope Promised*

DAY 4   27
*The Hope of a Savior*

DAY 5   31
*Born Into a Living Hope*

DAY 6   35
*Hope Forevermore*

*Weekly Reflection*   38

## WEEK TWO
## PEACE

DAY 1   41
*Candle Lighting Day
Scripture Memory*

DAY 2   45
*Perfect Peace*

DAY 3   49
*The Prince of Peace*

DAY 4   53
*Peace on Earth*

DAY 5   57
*He is Our Peace*

DAY 6   61
*Everlasting Peace*

*Weekly Reflection*   64

## WEEK THREE
## JOY

DAY 1   67
*Candle Lighting Day*
*Scripture Memory*

DAY 2   71
*Delighting in Creation*

DAY 3   75
*Joy Everlasting*

DAY 4   79
*Joyful Expectation of*
*the Coming Savior*

DAY 5   83
*Joyful in Life and Death*

DAY 6   87
*Joy Will Overtake Them*

Weekly Reflection   90

## WEEK FOUR
## LOVE

DAY 1   93
*Candle Lighting Day*
*Scripture Memory*

DAY 2   97
*For God So Loved*
*the World*

DAY 3   101
*A Story of Love*

DAY 4   105
*The Perfect Gift*

DAY 5   109
*The Great Sacrifice*

DAY 6   113
*The Culmination*
*of God's Love*

Christ Candle   116

Weekly Reflection   118

What is the Gospel?   120

# THE ADVENT CANDLE LIGHTING TRADITION

The lighting of Advent candles is a tradition practiced worldwide, but where did it come from? And why might we practice it today? The earliest roots of lighting Advent candles are unknown, but marking the birth of Jesus with a purposeful practice fits well into the Church calendar. The worldwide Church has a similar time of remembrance called Lent, which commemorates the death and resurrection of Jesus in the forty days leading up to Easter. So it seems natural to mark Jesus's birth with a weeks-long celebration as well.

We see Advent celebrations mentioned as early as 380 AD in a document from a church leadership meeting called the Council of Saragossa. The first Advent wreath and candles were used in Germany in 1839. There, a Lutheran minister who took care of orphaned children made a wreath out of a wheel and placed twenty white candles and four red candles on it. A white candle was lit each weekday, and a red candle was lit each Sunday in the four weeks leading up to Christmas.

Eventually, this idea spread, and the traditional Advent wreath with one candle for each Sunday of the Advent season (and optionally, a Christ candle at the center to be lit on Christmas Day) was born. Often, the Advent wreath that holds the candles is adorned with evergreen branches. The evergreen, which is vibrantly alive, even in the depths of winter, reminds us that God is eternal, and in Him, we too have everlasting life. The wreath is a circle that has no beginning and no end, reminding us that God always has been and always will be.

Each of the candles is symbolic and encourages us to remember the first coming of Christ and look forward to His second coming in a unique way. The candles represent hope, faith, joy, and peace. The optional fifth candle is called the Christ candle and represents Jesus. In this study, we will spend four weeks diving deep into each of the first four candles. Jesus will be the central focus of every week of study. Advent begins on the fourth Sunday before Christmas. On that Sunday, the hope candle is lit. On the second Sunday, both the hope and faith candles are lit, and this pattern continues through the Advent season.

Each week, when a candle is lit, the flicker of the flame reminds us that Jesus is the Light of the World. His first coming shines in the darkness, lighting the path to a relationship with God the Father and illuminating His plan and purpose through the work of the Holy Spirit. And we await His second coming when He will light the world with His glory (Revelation 22:5).

John 1:4-5 says, "In him was life, and that life was the light of men. That light shines in the darkness, and yet the darkness did not overcome it." This is what Advent season is all about, celebrating the light in the darkness—Jesus.

WEEK ONE / DAY ONE

## CANDLE LIGHTING DAY

# hope

*Today, we will light the hope candle. Hope is believing that what you desire may come to fruition. It is trusting that there are better things ahead. Christians, in particular, have a special relationship with hope.*

*Read 2 Corinthians 4:16-18, Isaiah 11:1-10, John 16:22, 1 Peter 1:3*

---

For centuries, Old Testament prophets declared the future hope of the arrival of the Messiah, Jesus. Old Testament prophets said that the Messiah would right all the wrongs in the world and bring true and lasting peace. Oh, how they hoped for Him! And Jesus did bring hope. All who believe in His death and resurrection have the hope of everlasting life! But Jesus gave even more hope than this. He also promised that after He was with His Father in heaven a while, He would return to earth again and make all things new. All tears would be wiped away; all pain would be gone; all sin would be removed from the earth.

Those who believe in Jesus have hope that through every trouble and tribulation of life, ahead of us is an eternity in the presence of Jesus, and we will partake in the new heaven and new earth He will bring forth. As you light the hope candle today, read the verses below, and reflect on the present and future hope we have in Jesus.

### PRAYER

*Lord, as we enter Advent season, we hold in tension two realities: heartbreak and hope. We have seen the harshness of sin and evil. And it is too close for comfort. Yet we also believe that You are close. We remember that You have not left us alone, subject to the sinfulness of the world, but instead, You sent us a Savior, Jesus. His first coming made a way for us to be forgiven of our sins. And we await His second coming when He will renew the earth and put an end to all sin and suffering. Yes, we see brokenness all around us, but one day we will see only blessedness. Though our hearts are distressed, we have hope. And it is this belief that fuels us to trust in You. Help us to fix our gaze on You this Advent season. Let our weary souls find rest in You as we wait in hope.*

*Amen.*

# HOPE

WEEK ONE
MEMORY VERSE

Blessed be the God and Father of our Lord Jesus Christ. Because of his great mercy he has given us new birth into a living hope through the resurrection of Jesus Christ from the dead

**1 PETER 1:3**

**HOPE HAS THE
FINAL WORD.**

WEEK ONE / DAY TWO

# The Hope of the World

*Read Genesis 1-3, Colossians 2:14-15*

It is not hard to see the deep darkness of the world around us. We see relationships that are broken beyond repair. We see diseases that dim the mind and cripple the body. We see global tragedy, pain, loss, and despair. Yes, we see the gloomy reality of the world. But do we also see the light breaking through? Because, even in the bleakest moments, God has given us hope.

When God created the world, He created a good world. He took unformed darkness and filled it with light, giving it structure and order. All the plants, animals, stars, and moon moved according to the structure He decreed, including a special creation who bore His image—man.

There was a special place in God's creation, called the garden of Eden, and in this garden, He placed the man and commissioned him to rule it and watch over it (Genesis 2:15). Eden also had rules. All the trees could be eaten from and enjoyed except one, the Tree of Knowledge of Good and Evil. God told the man that if he ate from it, he would surely die.

The creation story continues when God gives the man a perfectly suited helper for him–a woman, Eve. She was also to work and rule the garden with the man. The man and woman lived in a shame-free, pain-free, sin-free world. They communed face to face with God, taking walks with Him in the idyllic garden He had created. It was perfection. Until it was not.

Suddenly as if out of nowhere, a serpent enters the story. He is not just an ordinary snake, for he can speak, reason, and approach the woman with a sinister plan. The serpent is the tempter or Satan (Revelation 12:9). He is the leader of a revolt against God. Where God created order, he desires chaos. What God calls good, he calls a lie. Where God sends His light, he seeks to bring darkness.

He does so today, and he did this with the man and the woman in the garden. He approached the woman and accused God of withholding goodness from her because He would not allow her to eat from the Tree of Knowledge of Good and Evil. The woman believed the tempter, and she took a bite from the forbidden fruit. Then she handed it to the man who did the same.

At that moment, sin entered the world. Nothing would be the same again. Adam and Eve immediately knew that the fruit was not good and the serpent had lied. But their sin could not be undone. God banished them from the garden. But before He did that, He cursed the ground they worked and gave them hard labor. However, His greatest curse was not pronounced on the sinful people but on Satan. Nevertheless, this curse brought with it an undeniable flicker of hope.

Genesis 3:15 says, "I will put hostility between you and the woman, and between your offspring and her offspring. He will strike your head, and you will strike his heel." The serpent had succeeded in bringing his destruction to mankind, and hostility between the serpent and man would remain. But, one day, an offspring of the woman would strike the serpent's head, delivering a fatal blow. And the serpent, along with all of his cohorts, would be defeated once and for all. God would erase our certificate of debt by nailing it to the cross, giving His life for ours (Colossians 2:14-15).

God's response to the first human sin is to offer hope. Life will not always be like this—the world is suffering under the curse of sin. One day, the tempter will be destroyed. And God Himself would send Jesus, the One who can and will defeat him. What does this mean for us today? It means that when we are tempted and when we sin and when we suffer from the sins of others, that is not the end of the story. There is still hope because Jesus has already come once, and He will one day come again. Hope has the final word. God has not left us to eternally suffer the effects of sin but has promised to send Immanuel, "God with us." It is during Advent that we wait and pray and hope in Him.

> ## IT IS DURING ADVENT
> THAT WE WAIT AND PRAY
> AND HOPE IN HIM.

*What does God's response to the first sin tell you about His character?*

*Read Romans 3:23-24. What do these verses tell you about yourself? What does it tell you about the hope you have in Christ?*

*What heartbreaks are you experiencing? What does it look like for you to hope in God as you face these circumstances?*

**HOPE, THIS GLORIOUS HOPE, RESTS IN JESUS.**

WEEK ONE / DAY THREE

# Hope Promised

*Read Isaiah 11, Matthew 9:35-36, Revelation 21:1-8*

We will do anything to avoid sitting in the ache of the wait. Waiting causes tension within. We long for what will be while wrestling with the discomfort of the present. But Advent is a time when waiting is brought front and center. During the Christmas season, we intentionally fix our eyes on heaven in remembrance of the hope Jesus brought when He first arrived. And then our eyes fall back down to the sometimes painful reality of life on earth, and we find ourselves eagerly awaiting when He will come again.

Millenia ago, Israel had a similar time of waiting for the first appearance of the Messiah, Jesus. Israel knew God had a special promise for them. He had given it to Abraham, confirmed it to Moses, and reaffirmed it to David. God chose Israel to bring hope to the world, and God called them to live holy lives dedicated to Him. But while they knew this promise, they did not yet see it fulfilled in their lives. As the years passed and the Messiah's arrival was not yet realized, they became disillusioned and began to place their hope in other gods and even in themselves.

Their idolatry and rebellion against God rightly angered Him, and He sent prophets to call the nation to return to waiting for and hoping in Him alone. One such prophet was Isaiah. Isaiah warned the nation of Israel, and specifically, King Ahaz, that if they did not return to faithfulness, God would allow them to be destroyed by the powerful nations of Assyria and Babylon (Isaiah 10:5-6). Isaiah said the Israelites would be like a great forest felled at the hand of the Lord. Where once stood strong and flourishing trees would be only flattened stumps. In our mind's eye, we can imagine this scene—an endless horizon of barren land—and in our souls, we can feel the weight of Israel's rebellion as a nation. It cost them almost everything.

Yet, in the wake of such a sobering message, Isaiah offered one of the most stunning promises of hope in the Old Testament. Because although the trees representing the nation of Israel would be axed down due to their sin, Israel would not be completely destroyed. There would be new growth shooting forth from one stump, the stump of Jesse, the father of David. From David's line would come a new King, a better King, to lead the nation from rebellion and destruction to a future full of faithfulness and hope.

In every way, He would be a King unlike any other. The Spirit of the Lord would rest on Him, He would be wise and understanding, He would execute justice, and He would be clothed with righteousness and faithfulness. He would be the long-awaited King who would finally usher Israel into the future hope they were promised. As a result of His reign, the knowledge of the Lord would cover the earth, the Lord would recover the remnant of His people, and the promise of hope would be fulfilled.

In this one man, this shoot, was the hope of the whole world. And hope did come, more than 700 years after Isaiah wrote about Him. Jesus came as promised. In His 33 years of life, He healed, restored, and preached the good news of the kingdom of heaven (Matthew 9:35). Everyone who came near Him beheld a glimpse of heaven on earth. Then He died. And hope seemed lost once again. But He did not stay dead, and even His death was a part of the plan of hope, for through it, He made a way for all people to have a relationship with God.

Once His earthly mission was complete, He left the earth and ascended to heaven. But before He left, He sent a helper, and He gave a promise. He left the world with hope. The helper is His Spirit, who is with all believers to continue the mission of bringing heaven down to us. And the promise was that He would come again soon to complete the fulfillment of every hopeful thing He said He would do.

Therefore, we do not wait for the promise in despair but in hope. Hope, this glorious hope, rests in Jesus. As we consider His humble entrance into the world as a baby this Advent season, may we also eagerly await the day He returns in glory as King (Revelation 21:1-8). Like the Israelites rested for centuries in the promise of the Messiah, may we rest in the hope of His second coming. We wait. We trust. We hope. This is Advent.

WE WAIT. WE TRUST. WE HOPE.

## THIS IS ADVENT.

*In the Old Testament, God often gave the Israelites promises of hope during periods of rebellion. What does this tell us about God?*

*Can you relate to the Israelites who were so weary of waiting and hoping that they turned away from God? How does today's study encourage you to keep waiting in hope?*

*Write a prayer asking God to help you hope in Him in the areas of life you are prone to despair.*

THE HOPE WE HAVE IN
THE COMING OF CHRIST
CAN NEVER FADE.

WEEK ONE / DAY FOUR

# The Hope of a Savior

*Read Matthew 1*

Hopelessness is believing there will never be relief from pain, heartache, or sorrow. It is to be convinced you are alone and will always be alone in your anguish. It is to conclude there are no better days ahead. What a grim picture of life hopelessness paints.

And hopelessness is not only a personal experience but has been felt collectively in various degrees by every man, woman, and child from the beginning of time. Because although God created the world to be lovely, the first man and woman invited sin into the world when they disobeyed God. And because of sin, God's lovely earth became loathsome. Sin filled people with hate, cities with sickness, and eyes with tears. It flooded the earth with darkness—deep darkness. And there was utter despair.

Who could possibly reckon with such darkness? Who could offer hope strong enough to overcome this pain? God could. And He promised He would. He promised His people would not be alone and would not be forgotten, even on the bleakest days. For centuries, they clung to that promise because it was a glimmer of hope—one piercing beam of light shining in the darkness. With hope, they waited. And waited. And waited.

And then, in Matthew 1, the waiting is over. Jesus left His exalted throne in heaven and came to earth, the lowliest place, on a mission of hope. God chose a young girl and asked her to carry and birth the Messiah. Mary said yes. And her betrothed, Joseph, also said yes to marrying her, though she was a virgin with child.

Joseph knew the promise: "Therefore, the Lord himself will give you a sign: See, the virgin will conceive, have a son, and name him Immanuel" (Isaiah 7:14). And he believed that Mary's baby would be Immanuel. Could it really be that the wait was over? Was God truly coming to save the broken world? Yes. Immanuel, "God with us," was coming. Hope was on the way.

And while we sometimes want to rush past Jesus's birth to His life and death, there is much hope present, even in His humble entrance into the world. We must stop here and lean in to what happened. What is the significance of Jesus being born of a virgin? Is this just a small detail of the story, or is there more to it? There is more—much more.

There has never been and will never be again any person born of a virgin. Jesus stands alone as the only man to come into the world through this immaculate design. He is set apart from every other person in all of time. The virgin birth of Jesus also gives us a hint at what it means that Jesus is Immanuel, "God with us." He is both of God and with man.

And finally, Jesus's virgin birth is the first peek we are given into the miraculous works Jesus will accomplish throughout His earthly life, as well as after His death and resurrection. Jesus's life on earth begins and ends with supernatural circumstances. His birth involves a stable, a star, and shepherds, yet those small details simply frame the bigger picture. His birth is extraordinary.

As we breathe in the wonder that is Jesus, born of a virgin, may our hope be renewed. Because although the Israelites awaited His arrival for centuries, He arrived right on time—no earlier, no later, glory incarnate in the fragility of a newborn baby. Countless people prayed and longed and hoped for this Savior. And they had not done so in vain. Hope came.

And hope would not disappoint because before He left the earth to return to heaven, He would do all that God promised He would. He would break chains, free the oppressed, lift the weary, heal the sick, and cast out demons. He would be beaten and broken and choose to lay His life down on the cross. He would allow the Father to place upon Him all the sins of the world. He would satisfy the wrath of God with His death.

Yet, He would not stay dead. He would defeat sin and death by rising again to life only three days after He was placed in a tomb. And although His earthly life gave hope to many, His death and resurrection offer hope to all still today. All who are burdened and bruised by the effects of sin are offered forgiveness in Him.

Therefore, the hope we have in the coming of Christ can never fade. No matter how dark our days on earth, the hope of heaven with Jesus shines like the sun before us—in pain, in sickness, in sorrow, in frustration, in disappointment, in sin, in shame. Our hope through all of life is Jesus.

## OUR HOPE

THROUGH ALL OF LIFE IS JESUS.

*What is significant about the virgin birth of Jesus?*

*Read Mary's prayer of praise in Luke 1:46-55. What do you notice about how Mary responds to the Lord? How might this impact how you respond to the Lord?*

*What does Jesus's arrival on earth as promised mean for you personally? How does it give you hope?*

**THIS IS HOPE THAT IS ALIVE!**

WEEK ONE / DAY FIVE

# Born Into a Living Hope

*Read Matthew 28:1-10, 1 Peter 1:3-5*

With God, hope is never lost, even when it seems that way. The birth of Jesus was promised, prophesied, and fulfilled to the joy of those who awaited His coming. The life of Jesus, though, left many confused. Messianic promises painted Jesus as a powerful ruler who defeated evil and released a flood of hope on a weary earth. Yet, instead of ascending to the throne as a king, He spent His time with outcasts and sinners. He did not seem powerful but lowly. And He often rebuked the leading religious scholars for their lack of knowledge. He was not at all what they expected.

Some believed in Him, but many, like the Pharisees, distrusted Him and desired His destruction. The Pharisees plotted to kill Jesus. Judas, one of Jesus's closest companions and one of the twelve disciples, agreed to help the Pharisees locate and arrest Jesus.

After Jesus's arrest, He was condemned to death on a cross by the Roman governor, Pilate, at the insistence of the Jewish people. Jesus was beaten and whipped until He was near death, then He was brought to Golgotha to finish His execution. Roman soldiers nailed Him to a cross. Jesus's once-committed disciples ran and hid, ashamed that their leader was dying such a shameful death. Many wondered how Jesus could have been the Messiah. He had not seemed to bring hope as promised but instead suffered and died. Yet, hope was not lost!

Three days after Jesus's death, the tomb where He was buried was found to be empty. In the first portion of Matthew 28, we read that angels appeared to Mary and Mary Magdalene, who had come to prepare Jesus's body for burial, to tell them Jesus was alive. Imagine the flutter of hope within them as they heard those words. Could it be true?

Then Jesus Himself appeared to Mary and Mary Magdalene, and they realized that indeed the angels' message was true. Jesus is no longer dead but is alive! Jesus has resurrected. And every hope that felt as though it had been shattered in His death was suddenly mended with His resurrected life. Hope was alive in Jesus!

This story is nothing short of astounding, but it is no small feat to understand the story's meaning. Even the disciples were confused about what Jesus's death and resurrection meant for the world. Much of the Scripture that follows was written after Jesus's resurrection and explains what this significant event means. One such passage is 1 Peter 1:3-5.

In this passage, Paul praises God for the wonderful gift of salvation through the cross. He explains that Jesus's resurrection not only meant that Jesus Himself defeated death but that all who believe in Him will also overcome death one day. Through the resurrection of Jesus, all who believe in Him are given a new birth. They are born again and given a new life. And this new life is one of living hope.

Because Christ is alive, we too shall have newness of life if we believe in Him. This is more than just hope. This is hope that is alive! And our hope is in the fact that because we have been born again, we are now born into the family of God. We are children of God and heirs of the promise of God. We will take part in the promised hope of Israel, and we will have a King who reigns over the entire earth with justice and goodness. We, as believers in Jesus, have the hope of eternity in heaven before us.

1 Peter 1:4 says that this hope is "imperishable, undefiled, and unfading." This hope cannot be stolen or changed. It will not fade. It is indestructible. We have a living, indestructible hope. And the most stunning part is that this truth depends wholly on God. By His mercy, He causes us to be born again, He keeps our inheritance of hope safe, and He guards us during our earthly life until we experience hope in eternity forevermore. The resurrection of Jesus happened by the power of God, and by God's grace and power, we join in that resurrection with Him. We are not left to the power of sin and darkness, for we are saved and will experience that salvation in full one day when Jesus calls us home with Him. No matter how dark our days on earth, the hope of Jesus shines like the sun before us.

Some perceived Jesus's death and resurrection as defeat, but it was anything but that. His death and resurrection were victory over sin and death, and the hope of salvation is made available to all who believe. Because Jesus is alive, we can be alive. We can hope. We can live as people who have eternal, heavenly hope. Praise be to God!

## BECAUSE JESUS

IS ALIVE, WE CAN BE ALIVE.

WE CAN HOPE.

*The Israelites believed the Messiah would rule and reign as an earthly king, but Jesus's mission looked different than they thought. What does this tell you about Jesus?*

*Read 1 Peter 1:3-5. Write down the promises this verse gives us about the living hope we find in Jesus. What is your role in receiving this hope?*

*Think about times in which you have experienced difficulty or hardship. What does 1 Peter 1:6-9 tell you about hope in these times?*

**WE WAIT WITH EXPECTANT HOPE FOR THAT DAY THAT IS COMING SOON.**

WEEK ONE / DAY SIX

# Hope Forevermore

*Read Titus 2:11-13, Revelation 21*

When our lives lack hope, we can think about increasing hope in our souls, a lot like growing plants in a garden. Hope, like seeds, starts small. And although its development and growth begin immediately after it has been planted, it may be quite a while before we see the proof poking through the dirt. The seed becomes a plant and grows slowly, inch by inch, leaf by leaf. It needs roots to sustain it through driving winds and pounding rain. Heat threatens to scorch it unless a devoted caretaker waters it daily. And the fullest fulfillment of what was once a seed is the bloom of the plant, the fruit, which is often last to appear. Hope does not spring up big and bold and beautiful in a single day. It is grown first within and then seen in the open. It is delicate. It needs attention and nurturing. It would succumb to the elements of life if it did not receive the proper care.

Yet, in this analogy, it is not we but God who is the gardener of hope. He plants it deep within us, His children. He tends to it, devotedly cares for it, and will not allow it to perish. We are simply the soil, eager to grow good things but incapable of sprouting a seed on our own. Let us look to Scripture where we can draw these conclusions about hope.

After Jesus's resurrection, He spent forty days teaching the disciples about His conquering sin and death through the cross and rising again to life. He told them that His mission on earth was not done yet. The risen Messiah would be the reigning King of the earth as promised. Yet this would not happen right now but one day in the future. Jesus then ascended to heaven, where He still sits today at the right hand of God, interceding for all believers. He sent His Spirit, the Holy Spirit, to comfort, guide, and teach believers how to live as witnesses. Jesus planted a seed of hope.

Today, it has been almost two millennia since Jesus ascended to heaven, leaving the earth with His Spirit and the promise that He would be back again. And we are still left waiting. But we wait in joyful hope, knowing that Jesus always has and always will keep His promises. As every single Old Testament prophecy of the first arrival of Jesus was fulfilled, so will all of the Old and New Testament prophecies of His second coming be fulfilled. God's Word and the Holy Spirit tend to our hope with care and comfort as it grows, despite the world's harsh conditions.

So, what does the Bible say about the second coming, also called the second advent, of Jesus? We could easily fill an entire study answering this question alone, but we can greatly simplify it in this way:

Between the first and second coming of Jesus, the earth will groan under the weight of sin and the chaos it has caused. The groans will grow louder as we come closer to Jesus's arrival. We will see war, famine, hatred, death, and evil all around us. We may feel as if all hope is lost and evil has won control of God's good earth. But then, at the right time and not a moment sooner, Jesus will appear in the sky and will come to earth to establish the rule of peace and righteousness throughout the world. He will crush the head of the serpent and cast him and all of his evil counterparts into a lake of fire where they will remain forever. Those who have not trusted in Jesus for salvation will be sentenced to eternity apart from God. And those who have accepted Him will enter into something new and glorious. Because our hope is rooted in Christ, it will stay firm through every trial and tribulation.

All of heaven and earth will be made new. And with Satan and all sin forever banished from the earth, it will be an earth unlike anything we have ever known. Revelation 21:3-4 says, "Then I heard a loud voice from the throne: Look, God's dwelling is with humanity, and he will live with them. They will be his peoples, and God himself will be with them and will be their God. He will wipe away every tear from their eyes. Death will be no more; grief, crying, and pain will be no more, because the previous things have passed away." Oh, how we ache and hope and wait for that day!

Titus 2:13 calls Jesus's second coming our "blessed hope," which means this hope is one that will bring blessings. The biblical definition of "blessed" is "to be in God's grace and favor." Those who are in Christ experience God's grace and favor now, but they also experience the effects of sin. When Jesus establishes the new heaven and new earth, believers in Christ will only experience blessing. This passage also says that we will receive this blessed hope when Christ appears in glory for His second coming. The Greek word for "appear" that was used in the original text is something at which to marvel. The word used is ἐπιφάνεια (*epiphaneia*), and we derive the English word "epiphany" from this Greek root word. Although Jesus has already come once, His second coming will be different. It will be the culmination, the final revealing, the epiphany of God's great plan and purpose for the world. One day, our hope will bloom fully through the second coming of Jesus.

We wait in hope for the second coming of Jesus because when He comes again, He will reveal in fullness the glory of God on the earth. He will do this by ridding the earth of sin and death and creating a new heaven and new earth that He will reign over in peace and justice. Through this epiphany moment, this culmination of all the promises of God in Christ as King, believers will enter into unending blessings under the favor and grace of God. There will be a beautiful, blossoming garden of hope. What a blessed hope indeed! As we let these truths sink into our hearts and minds, we wait with expectant hope for that day that is coming soon.

*Consider how we have traced the theme of hope throughout Scripture from creation to Revelation this week. What have you learned about God's redemptive plan by studying in this way?*

*Read Revelation 21, and write a description of the new heaven and new earth in your own words.*

*Read Revelation 22:20. Write a prayer expressing your hope that Jesus will come again soon.*

# WEEK ONE REFLECTION
REVIEW ALL PASSAGES FROM THE WEEK

*Summarize the main points from this week's Scripture readings.*

*What did you observe from this week's passages about God and His character?*

*What do this week's passages reveal about the condition of mankind and yourself?*

*How do these passages point to the gospel?*

*How should you respond to these passages? What specific action steps can you take this week to apply them in your life?*

*Write a prayer in response to your study of God's Word. Adore God for who He is, confess sins He revealed in your own life, ask Him to empower you to walk in obedience, and pray for anyone who comes to mind as you study.*

WEEK TWO / DAY ONE

## CANDLE LIGHTING DAY

# peace

*The Peace candle is called the angel's candle, and it represents God's peace proclaimed by the angels in Luke 2:14. When Christ was born, the angels declared to the shepherds how Jesus had come to bring peace on earth. However, this was not the first time that God's peace had come to earth. God designed the world to be in perfect peace, but sadly, sin broke this peace.*

Read Luke 2:14, Romans 5:1

---

Now, sinners do not have peace with God or with one another. But in His grace, God promised to restore His perfect peace through His Son, Jesus. Through Jesus's sacrifice on the cross, Jesus forgives our sins and satisfies God's wrath, giving us lasting peace with God. But one day, Christ will come again and restore the whole world to a place of everlasting peace. As we light this candle, we rejoice over the peace that we have been given through Christ, and we rejoice over the peace that is to come when God restores all brokenness and unrest.

### PRAYER

*Dear God, our world is broken and full of unrest and disorder. We experience people hurting people, countries at war, and conflict within our communities. We long for this earth to be a place of peace, rest, and harmony. But while our world is dark, we light this candle to remember You are our God of peace. We praise You for sending our Prince of Peace, Jesus, who came to bring us peace with You through His death and resurrection. We praise You for giving us the Spirit who supplies us with daily peace. Remind us of Your perfect peace in this Advent season. May we find comfort knowing that one day we will experience a future of complete and lasting harmony. Until then, we rest in the peace we have through Your Son, Jesus.*

*Amen.*

# PEACE

WEEK TWO
MEMORY VERSE

Therefore, since we have been declared righteous by faith, we have peace with God through our Lord Jesus Christ.

**ROMANS 5:1**

**CHRIST WILL RETURN AND RESTORE THE WORLD BACK TO A PLACE OF PEACE.**

WEEK TWO / DAY TWO

# Perfect Peace

*Read Genesis 1, Genesis 3*

Before the world began, darkness surrounded the land. Tumultuous seas covered the earth. Then God spoke four words: "Let there be light" (Genesis 1:3), and the Lord began to form order in the world. Light and dark became balanced, and the seas were separated and made calm. By His goodness and grace, God placed trees and plants to provide abundance and made animals and humans to share in this abundance. Everything that God made was good, holy, and perfect. The world was the epitome of peace.

All that God made lived in perfect harmony. Humans and animals dwelled with one another with no fear of harm or mistreatment. Animals dwelled with one another with no desire for domination or attack. Adam and Eve dwelled with one another with no conflict or tension. The relationship between God and man rested in perfect harmony as well. Genesis 3:8 tells us that God walked in the garden with Adam and Eve. God shared an intimate relationship with Adam and Eve, with no limitations. But sadly, this perfect peace experienced in Eden would soon change forever.

When the serpent tempted Adam and Eve to take from the forbidden tree, sin entered into the world. Sin broke the perfect peace of Eden and brought chaos and disorder. We learn from Genesis 3:14-19 just how this peace was broken. Hostility was promised between the serpent and Eve's offspring. The perfect relationship between Adam and Eve broke as sin brought conflict, division, and tension into marriage. Adam's once joyful work was replaced with toilsome work, and Eve would endure painful child labor. But the worst part was that the relationship between God and man changed forever.

Adam and Eve likely experienced feelings of guilt and shame that were not present before sin. They went from once walking with God to hiding from God (Genesis 3:8). While they once dwelled with God in Eden, they were now exiled from the garden and removed from God's presence. The brokenness we see from sin shows us how sin changes the relationship between God and man. Sin breaks the perfect peace between God and man because sin cannot coexist with a holy God. Not only does sin separate God and man, but there is wrath between God and man because of sin. And God's wrath toward sin is just, for we rebel against a Holy God, and our sin deserves to be punished.

This lack of peace between God and man would be hopeless if God did not provide a glimmer of hope. In Genesis 3:15, we read how a promised offspring would come from Adam and Eve who would crush the serpent's head. Through this promise, Adam and Eve were given hope that their offspring would defeat sin and restore peace once again. But the hope of this offspring seems grim when Adam and Eve's children bring violence instead of peace. One of their children, Cain, selfishly murders his younger brother. It is clear that this offspring is not the one who will bring restoration. So who will?

Adam and Eve's contentious offspring paves the way for the true offspring, the true man of peace, Jesus Christ to come. Through Jesus's death and resurrection, Christ satisfied God's wrath. For those of us who believe in Jesus, the satisfaction of God's wrath means that we have been reconciled to God and have peace with God through Christ. We have peace as believers because of Christ's forgiveness, for we no longer fear punishment for our sins. Adam and Eve may have brought unrest and disorder, but by His grace, God made a way to restore rest and peace through Christ.

Today, we live in a world without peace. Creation is in disorder as we experience destructive storms, drought, and other natural disasters. Animals no longer live in harmony but fight against one another, devouring and defeating the weakest. Tension and conflict reside between people, and as a result, we experience war, oppression, and violence. The disorder and unrest of our world cause us to crave the peace that once existed in the garden. But as believers, we can survey the unrest around us with great hope. One day, Christ will return and restore the world back to a place of peace. He will remove all conflict, evil, tension, brokenness, and pain. Sin will be permanently removed from the earth, causing everything to be in harmony once again.

On the days when peace seems out of reach, this is the hope we have. The peace that is between God and us through Christ is a picture of the peace that will exist for all of creation one day. Unrest will not be a reality forever, for Christ will return to set all things right. And when He does, there will only be everlasting peace.

> **UNREST WILL NOT BE A REALITY FOREVER, FOR CHRIST WILL RETURN TO SET ALL THINGS RIGHT.**

*What does God's plan and promise to restore peace say about His character?*

*In what ways do you feel a lack of peace today?*

*How does knowing that God will restore peace comfort you in today's world of unrest?*

# THE PRINCE OF PEACE HAS COME.

WEEK TWO / DAY THREE

# The Prince of Peace

*Read Isaiah 9:1-7, Isaiah 53*

Little children love stories of princes and princesses. There is something so magical about watching the prince ride in on his horse and save the damsel in distress. Even as we grow older, we gravitate toward stories and movies of rescue. Living in a broken world, we crave justice and a way to escape the darkness around us. Advent is a season of waiting, and like a princess waiting for her rescue, we too are waiting to be rescued from this place of unrest. But as we wait, we are reminded that God has not left us without rescue. God has sent us Jesus, our Prince of Peace, to come to rescue us and restore peace to the world.

In the Old Testament, God's people were hungry for rescue. After rejecting obedience to God, the Israelites found themselves in exile. The Promised Land of peace God had graciously given them was ripped from their hands and destroyed. The nations around them held them in captivity and oppression. But in God's faithfulness, God rescues Israel by bringing them out of exile, even though they did not deserve His grace. Although they have returned, Israel's land is broken, and they are a tired and wounded people. Out of His kindness and grace, God uses prophets to bring hope to Israel. Through these prophecies, God promises a servant to rescue them and restore Israel to a place of peace.

In Isaiah 9:1-7, God promises that a child will be born to restore Israel's brokenness. Among other names revealing His character and purpose is the name Prince of Peace. This man will be a Prince of Peace in multiple ways. Isaiah 9:4-5 reveals how this man would lift Israel's oppression. He would remove the burden of oppression given to them by their enemies, trading war for peace. This prophecy reflects the prophecy of Isaiah 2:2-4, in which the promised servant would settle disputes among the nations and remove war for Israel, trading in objects of war for peaceful farm tools.

Isaiah 9:6 tells us how the government will be upon the shoulders of this man. As the Prince of Peace, this man will take control of the government with kindness and humility, administering lasting peace to the nation of Israel. Isaiah 9:9

reveals how this Prince of Peace will establish a kingdom of peace. His dominion would not just cover Israel but the whole earth, providing peace and prosperity that will never end.

However, the peace this man promises to provide goes deeper than freedom from oppressive rulers and nations for Israel. The word for "peace" in the passage is *shalom*. This *shalom* peace not only means an absence of conflict or trouble but is a positive blessing, particularly through a right relationship with God. This promised Prince would bring *shalom* to mankind by releasing sinners from their bondage to sin. He would provide a way for mankind to experience a right relationship with God.

Isaiah 53 tells us how this man would provide peace. We learn of a Suffering Servant who will experience much pain and agony on behalf of mankind. This man will experience the opposite of peace, as those around Him despise and reject Him, verbally and physically abusing Him. We learn in Isaiah 53:4-5 that this Suffering Servant will receive this pain for our sake, allowing Himself to be pierced and crushed for our iniquities, bearing our sin and shame so we could have peace.

Both the Prince of Peace and Suffering Servant referenced in these passages are Jesus Christ. By willingly dying on the cross, Jesus took on the punishment for our sins. Jesus experienced oppression so we could be freed from oppression. He experienced unrest so we could experience rest. He experienced God's wrath so we could have God's peace.

The peace that God has provided through Christ is a gift of grace. Just as God provided freedom and restoration for Israel out of the abundance of His grace, so has God given us freedom and restoration out of the abundance of His grace. Isaiah 26:12 tells us, "Lord, you will establish peace for us, for you have also done all our work for us." There was no way for us to restore the peace that was lost due to our sinful rebellion. There was no way for us to be reconciled in our relationship to God on our own. Jesus is our Prince of Peace who stepped in and sacrificed Himself so we could know everlasting peace.

God is both the initiator and fulfiller of true and lasting peace. Often, we can look for other ways to experience peace outside of God. While God has given us good gifts to bring us peace, like the creation around us or relaxing remedies, those gifts do not compare to the peace that God brings. Instead of looking to the things of this world for peace, we must come to the Prince of Peace, our God of peace, who will calm our hearts and give us rest. In God's presence is a peace that surpasses all understanding (Philippians 4:7).

As followers of Christ, we have been rescued from sin and death and will one day experience full rescue as Jesus returns to conquer sin and death once and for all. May this promised rescue bring us hope in this Advent season. The Prince of Peace has come, and indeed He will come again.

## THE PEACE THAT GOD HAS PROVIDED THROUGH CHRIST IS A GIFT OF GRACE.

*How does Christ being the Prince of Peace bring you comfort?*




*What does God being the initiator and fulfiller of peace say about His grace?*




*Where do you often go for peace? How can you come to God first to experience His peace?*

**WE ARE USED BY GOD
TO BRING HIS PEACE
INTO THE PRESENT.**

WEEK TWO / DAY FOUR

# Peace on Earth

*Read Luke 2:1-14*

Christmas is meant to be a time of rejoicing over our Savior, born to bring us peace. However, it can be hard to sing of peace when the world feels anything but peaceful. We are reminded of the Christmas hymn "I Heard the Bells on Christmas Day" that reads, "And in despair I bowed my head: 'There is no peace on earth,' I said, 'For hate is strong, and mocks the song of peace on earth, good will to men.'" These words resonate with us because we know what it is like to live in a world of hate rather than harmony. But as followers of Jesus, we do not have to despair even though our world is dark. Peace has come to earth, and this peace is here to stay.

The beloved Christmas story of the shepherds and angels reminds us that peace has come. As the shepherds attend their flocks, an angel appears to them, proclaiming that a Savior has been born. Soon, the angel is joined with a multitude of angels singing, "Glory to God in the highest heaven, and peace on earth to people he favors!" (Luke 2:14). This baby who has been born is the Prince of Peace, prophesied many years ago. He is also the Savior, the Messiah, the Lord. The fact that the angels proclaimed Jesus is Lord reveals how Jesus is God in the flesh. The God of peace has taken on human flesh and come to earth as the embodiment of peace on earth.

As we look to the proclamation of this peace, we notice that this peace is exclusive. The angels have not declared that this peace is for everyone but for those whom God favors. What makes this peace so exclusive is that this peace represents the peace between God and man. Jesus, our Prince of Peace, would soon make a way for God's wrath to be satisfied, reconciling sinners in their relationships with God and bringing peace between them. But this beautiful and remarkable gift of peace with God is for those who trust and believe in Jesus. Only those who come to faith in Christ can know the peace that Christ brings. To experience God's peace, we must have a relationship with the God of peace, and this relationship is only made possible through salvation in Christ.

As we look around our world today, we understand why the angels proclaimed that peace is not a reality for all people. Our world today has broken systems, oppression, and violence. Sin prevents peace from being on the earth, and people contribute to the conflict and injustice of our world because of their sin. Even unbelievers who desire peace cannot know true peace or be conduits of true peace without Christ. But as believers, we can sing songs like "I Heard the Bells on Christmas Day" and others resonating peace with hope.

As followers of Christ, we have experienced the peace of which the angels speak. By Christ's grace and forgiveness, we have been given peace with God. This peace should humble us and stir within us a deep gratitude for Christ. It is a gift of grace to have the wrath between God and us satisfied and to know the God of Peace intimately. We can be cheered, even in the darkness of our world, knowing that God's peace is a light amidst the darkness. It exists in us through Christ. And one day, Christ will return, bringing peace upon the earth in its fullness.

While we must wait to experience the fullness of God's peace, we have God's peace in the present. Before ascending into heaven, Jesus told His disciples, "Peace I leave with you. My peace I give to you. I do not give to you as the world gives. Don't let your heart be troubled or fearful" (John 14:27). Jesus has not left us in a world of unrest without His peace. Through the Holy Spirit inside of us, we have Christ's peaceful presence with us daily and can experience His peace deeply as we rest in the Spirit and ask the Spirit to help us feel His peace.

The Holy Spirit empowers us to share the message of God's peace. The world may be dark, but we act as lights for Christ as we share how true peace can be found in Christ. Just as the angels proclaimed the message of God's peace, so are we to proclaim the same message by sharing the gospel with others. If we want others to come to know God's peace, we not only need to share the gospel but also reflect the peace of God through our conduct and speech. May we extend kindness and grace to others as peacemakers and refrain from stirring up conflict (Matthew 5:9). To do so, we must let the peace of Christ rule in our hearts as we draw near to God in prayer and remain in His Word. Daily we are to walk by the Spirit, relying on His power to produce the fruit of peace.

One day, Christ will return to bring lasting peace on earth, but for now, we are used by God to bring His peace into the present. Let us rest in the peace we have through the Spirit and rely on His power alone to be peacemakers in a world of unrest. The peace of God given to us through Christ is the remedy for our broken world, so let us joyfully share the gospel, spreading God's peace to all corners of the earth.

LET US JOYFULLY SHARE THE GOSPEL, SPREADING GOD'S PEACE TO ALL CORNERS OF THE EARTH.

*How can we sing of God's peace during Christmas time with hope?*

*How does today's passage encourage you to share the gospel?*

*How can you be a peacemaker this week?*

## AS BELIEVERS, WE HAVE FULL ACCESS TO GOD THROUGH THE SPIRIT.

WEEK TWO / DAY FIVE

# He is Our Peace

*Read Ephesians 2:14-18, 2 Corinthians 5:17-21, Romans 5:1*

When conflict arises between us and a friend, there is a lack of peace. While once our relationship was harmonious, something has happened to break the peace between us. Now, what exists is bitterness, hurt, distance, and tension. In order for our relationship with this friend to be restored, we need to be reconciled. We need to come back together, forgive one another, and mend the relationship that was broken. Once this occurs, peace and harmony are restored. This picture of conflict reflects the relationship between God and man. Because of sin, there is a chasm between God and man that cannot be satisfied by our own doing. But through Christ's death and resurrection, those who believe and trust in Jesus receive reconciliation with God. Jesus is our peace who has brought us peace with God (Ephesians 2:14-18).

By taking on our sins and dying on the cross, Jesus took the punishment that we deserve for our rebellion against God. He took on God's wrath and satisfied that wrath so that we could be free, reconciled to God (2 Corinthians 5:18). This gift is called justification—through Christ's sacrifice, we are cleared from our sinful record and declared righteous before the Lord. Romans 5:1 tells us that since we have been justified, we have peace with God through Jesus. Because Jesus took on God's wrath and satisfied His wrath, there is now only peace between us and the Lord when we accept Him as our Savior. We must no longer fear condemnation because of our sin.

The reconciliation we have received from Christ also grants us complete access to God. Before Jesus took His last breath, the temple curtain was torn in two. This curtain previously separated God's earthly dwelling place in the temple—a place called the Holy of Holies—and the area where men could gather. The curtain tearing symbolized how Jesus's sacrifice on the cross broke down the barrier between God and man. Those who believe in Jesus have the wall of hostility torn down that once separated them from God, allowing for complete and unhindered access to Him. The relationship that mankind experienced with God before the fall is restored, although the fullness of that relationship will not be fully known until Christ returns. As believers, we have a relationship with God with no barriers (Romans 8:39). Because of Christ's sacrifice and grace, we are tethered to Christ, our Savior, forever.

As believers, we have full access to God through the Spirit. This means that we are welcome to approach God in prayer and never need to fear coming to Him. A little child might be afraid to approach his father because he knows he did something wrong and fears his father's anger. But those of us who have been reconciled to God never need fear in approaching our heavenly Father. When we sin and falter in our obedience, we grieve that sin and certainly do not take the Lord's kindness as a token to sin. But, as His children, we can approach Him with complete confidence, remembering His immeasurable forgiveness, grace, and mercy.

What also makes our reconciliation special is that Christ's peace makes the peace between us and believers possible. Jesus not only broke down the wall of hostility between us and God but also between us and others. Throughout Scripture, there was conflict between Jews and Gentiles (non-Jews). But God's divine plan was to bring peace between these two peoples, breaking down the wall of hostility between them so both could receive grace and forgiveness through Christ. Instead of two separate groups, Christ brought both groups together and made them one, resulting in peace.

And by His grace, that is what Jesus does for us today. Followers of Jesus are one unified body in Christ, regardless of what we look like, where we come from, or what we have done. As the body of Christ, we work together to bring the message of reconciliation—the gospel—to the world. However, we can hinder the gospel's message when we fail to have peace with one another. At times, we can fail to be peacemakers by breeding division and animosity amongst other believers. If the watching world does not see peace between believers, how will they desire to know God's peace?

We do not receive God's peace then refuse to share that peace with others. Instead, we are to bear with one another in love and make every effort to keep the unity of the Spirit through the bond of peace (Ephesians 4:2-3). We treat others with kindness and respect, even when we disagree with them or are hurt by them.

In this Advent season, let us praise Jesus for being our peace and making it possible for us to experience God's peace with Him and those around us. We were once enemies of God, but now we are friends of God. What a reason to rejoice!

---

BEAR WITH ONE ANOTHER

## IN LOVE.

*How does your reconciliation with God comfort you when you sin?*




*How do you struggle to have peace with other believers? Are there relationships you need to reconcile so there is peace in the body of Christ?*




*Spend some time in prayer, thanking Jesus for being your peace and providing you peace with God.*

**THIS WORLD OF UNREST IS NOT OUR FINAL HOME.**

WEEK TWO / DAY SIX

# Everlasting Peace

*Read Revelation 21*

Finding peace in the Christmas season can often be difficult in light of trials and troubles. For some of us, peace feels out of reach because we have broken relationships within our families. Or maybe someone we know is sick, and it is hard to feel at rest knowing about their struggles. How can we have peace when the season feels sorrowful and hopeless? Advent looks to Christ's first coming, but there is also a second Advent to come. One day, Jesus will return, ushering in the fullness of God's peace that was lost at the fall. Our future eternity of peace encourages our peace in the present.

Revelation 21 paints for us a picture of the peace to come, but first, we must consider what has caused this peace to occur. Throughout the chapter, we see evidence of a new creation. John begins this chapter by saying he saw a new heaven and a new earth, for the first earth had passed away. The Lord says, "Look, I am making everything new" and "It is done!" (Revelation 21:5-6). These words from the Lord reveal how the world has been transformed. God's work of restoration is complete, for Christ has conquered sin and death once and for all.

Revelation 21:4 tells us, "He will wipe away every tear from their eyes. Death will be no more; grief, crying, and pain will be no more, because the previous things have passed away." Though the present is painful, there is a future ahead where suffering will be no more. Whatever it is that gives you a lack of peace today will vanish. No more will the burden of sickness, disorder, and death weigh upon us. No more will we grieve the injustice and oppression that infiltrate our world. When it is difficult to feel at peace in the present, look to the promised peace to come. This world is not our permanent home—there is a new creation coming when God will make all things new. And when sin and darkness press in, remind yourselves of the truth that "the God of peace will soon crush Satan under your feet" (Romans 16:20).

But we ask, "What will our future peace look like?" It will look like a place of complete harmony. Isaiah 11:6-9 promised how the new creation would involve once dangerous animals dwelling with harmless animals. This picture of harmony reflects the harmony that will exist for all of creation. There will be no war, no conflict, no violence. What the Prince of Peace is promised to do in Isaiah 9:7 will also come to pass. Jesus, our Prince of Peace, will establish His dominion on the earth, and His dominion will be full of lasting prosperity. The new creation will be a place of abundance like Eden, but better, as God's kingdom of peace will cover the entire world. The rule of our Prince of Peace contrasts the rulers that bring unrest to our world today. In the new creation, we will never have to fear being in a world with unjust, unwise, or oppressive rulers. Jesus, our Prince of Peace, will rule with perfect justice and righteousness.

And most of all, we will experience the fullness of our peace with God. Revelation 21:3-4 reveals how God will come to dwell fully on the earth. The kind of relationship Adam and Eve had with God before the fall will be the kind of relationship we will have with God. We will experience the joy of being in God's unhindered, physical presence. God will be our God, and we will be His people forever.

There is a future of promised peace for God's people, but what does this mean for us now? Jesus says in John 16:33, "I have told you these things so that in me you may have peace. You will have suffering in this world. Be courageous! I have conquered the world." Personal suffering, as well as the suffering of this world, can leave us anxious and weary, but Christ has given us His peace. We can have peace even though we walk in a world of suffering because Jesus has conquered this world of suffering. He rules and reigns over this world and has complete control. While He will come back to rule over the earth fully, He reigns even now as He holds the world in His hands. When the circumstances of this life leave us shaken, we can find rest in our Prince of Peace. And as we rest in Christ's peace in the here and now, we can look with hope to the peace that is to come.

This world of unrest is not our final home. Jesus will return, and when He does, we will experience a new creation of everlasting peace. As we await that day, we rest in the hope of that peace we have now through the Spirit. May this Advent season remind you of Christ's first coming but also the second advent that is to come, full of peace unending.

> **MAY THIS ADVENT SEASON** REMIND YOU OF CHRIST'S FIRST COMING BUT ALSO THE SECOND ADVENT THAT IS TO COME, FULL OF PEACE UNENDING.

*How can the future peace to come encourage you when the present is difficult?*

*What excites you about dwelling in God's presence fully?*

*How can you rest in Christ's peace when you are afraid?*

# WEEK TWO REFLECTION
REVIEW ALL PASSAGES FROM THE WEEK

*Summarize the main points from this week's Scripture readings.*

*What did you observe from this week's passages about God and His character?*

*What do this week's passages reveal about the condition of mankind and yourself?*

*How do these passages point to the gospel?*

*How should you respond to these passages? What specific action steps can you take this week to apply them in your life?*

*Write a prayer in response to your study of God's Word. Adore God for who He is, confess sins He revealed in your own life, ask Him to empower you to walk in obedience, and pray for anyone who comes to mind as you study.*

WEEK THREE / DAY ONE

## CANDLE LIGHTING DAY

# joy

*The joy candle represents delight in Jesus's birth and salvation. We light the joy candle to celebrate Jesus's first coming and look forward to His second coming. The eternal Son of God entered the world and came near to us. His arrival fulfilled the Lord's covenant commitment to His people because Jesus was the Savior. He rescued us from our sinful nature and restored our relationship with God the Father. He healed us from the curse of disobedience and gave us a new identity. Soon, Jesus will descend from heaven again to completely destroy the power of evil and establish His eternal kingdom on earth. This good news brings us true joy—not the temporary happiness worldly indulgences offer.*

*Read Psalm 100, Philippians 4:4-5*

---

Biblical joy is more than an attitude that varies with circumstances. Instead, it is a confident cheer in Jesus's presence. Scripture echoes this sentiment in examples throughout redemptive history. In the Old Testament, we see the Israelites rejoice in God's favor in the midst of wandering and trials. In the New Testament, we see the Apostle Paul call believers to rejoice in the Lord's grace when he was imprisoned. These examples show how being rooted in God's promises affects our disposition in any situation. This advent season, may joy in the Savior's glory and our future glory through Him capture us, and as we light the candle, let us enter into this joy with glad hearts.

## PRAYER

*Dear Father, You are the God of joy. Your happiness is everlasting, and You desire to delight in us. We confess that we have not found satisfaction in You. We have rejected Your cheerful invitation to experience bliss in Your presence. We prioritize busyness, social life, and work over You, Lord, and come to You dissatisfied. Holy Spirit, we thank You for drawing us back and reminding us of Christ's fulfillment. We are grateful for Jesus's forgiveness and consistent companionship. Help us experience joy in intimacy with You. We want to be people who rejoice in our salvation and in our destiny with Christ. We plead for the Holy Spirit to give us this elation for all circumstances. When we grieve the world's brokenness, help us hold both the pain and joy in tension. May we know that our sorrow is not in vain but will lead us to praise.*

*Amen.*

JOY

WEEK THREE
MEMORY VERSE

Rejoice in the Lord always.
I will say it again: Rejoice!
Let your graciousness be
known to everyone.
The Lord is near.

**PHILIPPIANS 4:4-5**

**GOD REPLACED THE OLD CREATION WITH THE NEW CREATION.**

WEEK THREE / DAY TWO

# Delighting in Creation

*Read Genesis 1:31 and Genesis 6:5-7*

A sculptor finds joy in his completed work of art. He stands back to marvel at the transformation. The once unformed and unpleasing clay is an object of beauty and purpose, reflecting the creativity and skill of its master. Like a sculptor expressing deep satisfaction in his work, God takes pleasure in His creation, and Scripture describes God's delight over His creation in Genesis 1:31. In the beginning, the cosmos were unordered and empty. The eternal God hovered over the void and gathered up the nothingness into His hands. He spoke and formed the galaxies. He molded and arranged the earth's mountains and seas. With ease, God made mankind, His own glorious image-bearers, from dull dust. When He finished forming the universe, God beheld it all, every texture, every color, and every particle, and He was happy. The Lord declared His art "very good" (Genesis 1:31). These words describe the perfection of creation. The world's beauty and function were as the Creator intended. Everything gave glory to God, and God rejoiced in intimate rest with His creation. The Lord shined His blessing on the first humans, and in response, they found joy in the presence of their Maker.

Unfortunately, mankind did not remain joyful toward God. Enticed by Satan, Adam and Eve no longer saw God as the source of complete satisfaction. They desired to taste counterfeit pleasures and consume temporary happiness. Adam and Eve sinned against God by eating the fruit of the tree which God forbade. As a result, they produced a population that inherited their disobedient nature. In Genesis 6:5-7, Scripture indicates that the wickedness of mankind grew and permeated hearts. Mankind was so depraved that men and women did and thought evil continuously. Sin corrupted God's masterpiece; all of the earth rebelled against the Maker's will and design. As a result, the Lord expressed grief and anger at the injustice. His concern was so great that the author of Genesis wrote that the Lord "regretted" creating mankind (Genesis 6:6). The use of this word did not mean to convey that God changed His disposition, for God remains the same forever. Rather, through the biblical author, the Lord was revealing His desire to enjoy His creation and His desire to make it right again. He would send a flood to wash away the wickedness. As a sculptor who throws out polluted clay, God would wipe out the pollution from His people.

God replaced the old creation with the new creation. In Genesis 6:8, we read that God preserved the faith in a man named Noah. God saved Noah, his family, and a pair of every kind of animal from the flood. A new creation emerged from the waters, and God's grief and anger diminished as justice was served. But, Noah was still sinful, and his joy in the Father would wane. Wickedness would spread once again. So, God's people continued to long for the Man who had true joy in the Father, the Man who would usher in a new creation completely dedicated to the Lord. Jesus Christ was this Man, full of joy. He constantly delighted in God and was pleased to do His will. Because of Jesus's perfect obedience, the Father rejoiced in His Son. Jesus did what Noah was unable to do. Fully righteous, Jesus took the punishment for our sin when He died on the cross. Because of His delight in the eternal Son, the Lord preserved Jesus from the grave. Jesus rose from the dead and brought an era of restoration to God's creation. And, He will one day return to fully restore all so that we, as God's creation, can live as He intended.

Through His saving work, we can live as God's workmanship, faithful image-bearers who honor the Lord and give Him glory (Ephesians 2:10). The Holy Spirit renews us from being dead in sin to having life with Christ when we place our faith in Jesus. Day by day, we change from distorted, broken, and ruined clay fragments to glorious reflections of God's power and love. As we pursue the beauty and purpose for which we were made, we begin to look like our Savior. We become more gentle, more patient, and more selfless. We increasingly discover pleasure and satisfaction in the Lord's presence. However, we will still wrestle with remnants of our past selves. We will become discouraged when the stains of sin continue to distort. We may think that God no longer delights in us or that He does so begrudgingly. But, we can rejoice, for God does not cease to rejoice in us. His joy toward us is eternal because it is rooted in the eternal plan of God. Before creation, throughout redemptive history and in the midst of our future sin, God continues to delight in us because His Son's righteousness covers us.

## THROUGH HIS SAVING WORK,
WE CAN LIVE AS GOD'S WORKMANSHIP.

*What do Genesis 1:31 and Genesis 6:5-7 reveal about God's character?*

*How has sin impacted your joy in God?*

*In what ways does knowing that Jesus delights in you affect your relationship with Him?*

## AN ETERNAL JUBILEE

WEEK THREE / DAY THREE

# Joy Everlasting

*Read Isaiah 61, Luke 4:16-21*

The air can seem different in December. The excitement for the holidays is palpable. Beyond peppermint hot chocolate and twinkling decorations, there is an unspoken invitation to partake in cheer, and everyone seems to welcome it. People look forward to resting from work and busyness; people want to feel joy! The Lord knew this. In fact, when we look at Scripture, we see that the Lord instructed His people to incorporate rhythms of rest into their lives.

In the Old Testament, God instituted the weekly Sabbath. He also called for a sabbatical year every seven years (Leviticus 25:3-7). It was a year of rest. The land would be revitalized as the soil's nutrients were restored over the course of the year. The people would cease from tending to the fields and feast on what naturally grew. After seven cycles of this sabbatical year, the people of God were then to observe the Year of Jubilee, an additional year of rest occurring every fifty years. It was the "year of the Lord's favor" where debts were canceled, slaves were freed, and land was returned to its original owners. It was a year of rest and restoration. It was a glimpse of the Father's heart and His plan of ushering in eternal Jubilee through Jesus. This is what the prophecy in Isaiah 61 tells us — there is One who will come and take care of our spiritual debt, free us from the enslaving power of sin, and restore creation to exceed its former glory in Eden.

The Israelites were familiar with this reference to Jubilee. They knew the values it communicated — the Jubilee law was to esteem freedom, rest, and restoration. The Israelites highly valued these principles. This is why it is particularly noteworthy that the prophecy in Isaiah 61 was given when it was given, just prior to Israel's Babylonian captivity. Israel was divided into two kingdoms, and spiritual purity was on the decline. Soon, God's people would endure judgment for their disobedience and idolatry in the form of captivity. Freedom, rest, and restoration would undoubtedly be their deep desires.

The prophet Isaiah pointed to the Messiah as the One who would give true freedom, rest, and restoration. He is the Anointed One, empowered by the

Spirit. He is the One who will heal the brokenhearted, proclaim liberty to the captives, comfort and provide for those who mourn, and offer clothes of righteousness instead of despair, a crown of beauty instead of ashes. Isaiah said that He would proclaim the year of the Lord's favor—the year of Jubilee. The people were eagerly waiting for this Messiah. They would be exiled, living as sojourners in a foreign land, longing for the fulfillment of this prophecy. But the prophecy would not be fulfilled for another 700 years.

Praise the Lord it was fulfilled! On that first Christmas day, the angel declared the "good news of great joy": the Messiah had come, just as He said He would, and the prophecy was fulfilled (Luke 2:10). He came into the world unassumingly, clothed in human flesh as a helpless baby. Yet, He grew and lived without sin because He was also fully God. In Jesus, every one of God's promises were met (2 Corinthians 1:20), even the one in Isaiah 61. Jesus actually says this Himself. A year into His public ministry, He entered a synagogue in His hometown and pointed back to this very prophecy in Isaiah 61. It was the Sabbath, and He read aloud from the scroll of the prophet Isaiah (Isaiah 61:1-2) and then said this: "Today as you listen, this Scripture has been fulfilled" (Luke 4:21). His audience that day were people who knew Him well because He had grown up in that very town of Nazareth. Yet, their amazement of His gracious words still led them to disbelief.

They had missed this glorious, gospel truth that the long-awaited Messiah had come. The anointed One was before them, proclaiming the year of the Lord's favor. But this time, it would not be just a year. No, the year of Jubilee that Jesus was ushering in was the age of salvation. It ushered in our reality in Jesus Christ today!

In Isaiah's prophecy, God said that His people would experience blessings upon their deliverance from captivity. They would return to the land given to them by God and prosper. They would no longer be slaves but priests. They would be free to serve the Lord and bring Him glory. Their houses would be rebuilt, and they would have plenty. They would experience freedom and joy, for the Lord had placed His love on them. He is a God who makes and keeps His covenants. And ultimately, it would all be for His glory.

While this prophecy was about the Israelites at that time, all of us in Christ know this to be true: in Him, we have been delivered from spiritual captivity. We are no longer slaves but sons and daughters of righteousness (Galatians 4:7). Now, we have the indwelling Spirit, and He empowers us to lay aside the sins that so easily entangle us. We are a royal priesthood (1 Peter 2:9), invited to serve God and participate in His ministry of reconciliation. He equips us to do this by giving us every spiritual blessing in the heavens (Ephesians 1:3). We are the Church, built on a firm foundation that cannot be shaken. In His presence, we enjoy true freedom (2 Corinthians 3:17). In His presence, we experience the fullness of joy (Psalm 16:11).

This Advent, may we consider the anticipation the people of God felt for the Messiah. May we remember that we too are merely sojourners in this land, and we are in our own season of waiting. Yes, we rejoice that the Savior has come, but we also long for the day when He will return and fully make all things new—an eternal Jubilee.

*The words of Isaiah 61 were offered prior to the Babylonian captivity. They were words of hope and joy that the people would reflect on while in exile. How do the promises of God in Scripture bring you hope and joy in your journey?*

*Write out all of the glorious things that the Messiah would do in Isaiah 61. How has He done this in your life? Spend some time offering up prayers of thanksgiving.*

*How does this fulfilled prophecy increase your joy in the Lord?*

**OUR DELIGHT IS SAFE IN CHRIST.**

WEEK THREE / DAY FOUR

# Joyful Expectation of the Coming Savior

*Read Luke 1:26-55*

A baby shower is a joyous event that celebrates a baby's expected arrival and a woman's transition into motherhood. We may have seen pictures of baby showers, showing images of colorful balloons, decadent desserts, and gifts all around. We may have even planned or attended a few of these ourselves and felt the happiness in the atmosphere. Despite whatever games or festivities are organized, the soon-to-be mother is the center of attention. People are excited in her presence. The coming delivery evokes thrill and elation. Smiles, laughter, and words of cheer surround the baby in her womb, and she rejoices in God's blessing. We see a similar jubilee in today's reading. The angel Gabriel greeted Mary with joy and called her "favored woman" (Luke 1:28). Unbeknownst to her, Mary was going to carry the Son of God. Though Mary was not likely given a baby shower to celebrate the news, she had great joy in the coming Savior.

Mary visited Elizabeth, her cousin, who also was to have a miraculous birth. Elizabeth was barren and old in age, but the Lord chose her to deliver the prophet, John, who would prepare the way for Jesus. Mary saw Elizabeth's rounded belly in the distance and called to her cousin. At Mary's greeting, Elizabeth's unborn child leaped within her and was filled with the Holy Spirit. Elizabeth praised God for His faithfulness and shouted, "Blessed are you among women, and your child will be blessed" (Luke 1:42)! Elizabeth rejoiced, and even the child "leaped for joy" within her at the Savior's coming and nearness. This awareness and delight in Jesus's presence was a gift from the Holy Spirit. Elizabeth went on to express joy in Mary's faith. God graciously gifted Mary the faith to take part in His plan. Elizabeth's words of encouragement comforted Mary and roused her to express her own joy with confidence.

Then, Mary sang. From the depths of her heart, she praised God for His care toward the humble and His victory over darkness. The proud, the unrepentant, and the unjust rulers of the age would fall at the Savior's hand. But, the reverent, the lowly, and the hungry would be exalted and satisfied in Jesus. Mary joined the chorus of Old Testament believers who trusted in the Lord. She mirrored the delight of the psalmist who wrote, "Then I will rejoice in the Lord; I will delight in his deliverance" (Psalm 35:9). She echoed the sentiment of Hannah, the mother of Israel's prophet, who said, "My heart rejoices in the Lord; my horn is lifted up by the Lord. My mouth boasts over my enemies, because I rejoice in your salvation" (1 Samuel 2:1).

This redemptive, historical joy in the Savior climaxed at the birth of Jesus. Though He was born amid meager conditions and was laid in an animal's feeding trough, people came with excitement to see God in the flesh, for the Savior had come. They showered him with gifts. The angels exclaimed the Lord's glory and danced in the skies. The celebration of Jesus's birth fulfilled the desires of God's people for so long. And, the praise of His nearness gives us a glimpse of the eternal joy that we will sing of forever.

Because of Christ's saving work, we can live with joyful expectation through the Holy Spirit in us. We should daily celebrate His accomplishment and His return to fully manifest His kingdom. When times of sadness and despair come, may we remember the stories of Mary and Elizabeth. When spiritual evil tries to steal our joy, we can find comfort that our delight is safe in Christ because He reigns. When we fall and seek the pleasures of this world, we can pray for true joy found in Christ alone. Throughout our days, let us smile, laugh, play, sing, and dance with confident joy and praise in the Lord most high!

> WE CAN PRAY FOR TRUE JOY FOUND
>
> **IN CHRIST ALONE.**

*What does Luke 1:26-55 reveal about God's character?*

*Are there circumstances in your life that are seeking to rob you of joy during this season? Say a prayer asking the Lord to work in those circumstances and help you to find true joy in Him alone.*

*How can you celebrate the joy of Jesus's birth this week?*

**JESUS IS THE REASON
FOR OUR JOY.**

WEEK THREE / DAY FIVE

# Joyful in Life and Death

*Read Hebrews 12:1-3, Psalm 30:4-5*

How easy it is to feel joy when life is going well. It is natural to rejoice in happiness when we receive a promotion or get engaged. We celebrate with excitement over a positive pregnancy test or when we close on a new home. We squeal when our kids are accepted into a good school or when the test for cancer comes back negative.

But what about when life is hard? What about the moments when you face pain and sorrow upon sorrow? Or when others mock you or betray you? Can you imagine your response if all your friends abandoned you while your enemies greedily condemned you? What if they accused you of crimes you did not even commit and sent you to die a criminal's death? Not many of us would be joyful then. Yet somehow, miraculously, Jesus was joyful even in His suffering. He did not drag His feet to Calvary, angry and bitter at His Father. He went joyfully to His death. He went willingly to the cross. He ran perfectly in the race set before Him. Though weak and weary from scrapes and scars, He endured in faith to His death.

That is not to say that Jesus was naive of what was to come or that He had an incredible tolerance for pain. It is not that He was indifferent about dying on a tree. Indeed, Scripture says He endured the cross, bravely bearing its injustice. He despised, disdained, and condemned its shame. He took on the complete humiliation of crucifixion, and yet, He did so with joy.

How could Jesus have joy in the midst of unjust persecution? How could He joyfully take up the instrument of His crucifixion? He did this out of great love for the Father and us. Jesus knew that through His death, we would be set free from the penalty of sin. He knew that as He hung exposed on the cross, He destroyed the power of shame for all who would believe in Him. He knew that in His suffering, God was working a grander plan of redemption. He saw the bigger picture and knew that salvation was only possible through His perfect sacrifice. He came to save, redeem, and restore what was broken—joyfully, through His death.

Not only this, Jesus knew that the grave could not hold Him. When He arose from the grave three days later, He triumphed once and for all over sin and death. As Jesus walked again with scars on His hands in the days following His crucifixion, He offered His followers a joy that surpasses worldly happiness. He offered them eternal life and peace with God; he offered them hope. He promised that death was no longer the end of our story, and He instead offered everlasting life to all who believed in Him. Now, this same Jesus sits at the right hand of the Father in Heaven, ruling over all. He offers the joy of salvation to all who believe in Him. He covers over our shame and draws near to us in our pain. He adopts us into God's family as sons and daughters, loving us, protecting us, and covering us with His perfection.

Jesus is the reason for our joy. As His followers, we are not promised lives free from trouble. Rather, in Christ, we are offered surpassing joy in knowing that God is with us in each trouble. Scripture reminds us that though our troubles may last for the night, His joy comes in the morning (Psalm 30:5). We can rest confidently, even in hardships, because our King is with us in the midst of every trial. We have eternal victory because of Jesus's life, death, and resurrection, for we are cleansed of all guilt and shame and covered by His perfect righteousness.

Since Jesus so joyfully endured the cross, we too can find strength and joy today. As Christians, we can follow our Savior by obeying God's Word, speaking kindly to others, and living lives of integrity and purity even when it is hard. We can joyfully take to heart the words of Hebrews 12:1-3 by resisting temptation, knowing that God's plans are greater. We can run our race with endurance and joyfully endure trials, knowing that God is with us, working good through it all. We can rejoice as we identify with the sufferings of Christ, even as others mock or malign us for our beliefs. We can find strength in His finished work on the cross so that we do not grow weary or give up (Hebrews 12:3). We can remember what is eternal as we are surrounded by a great cloud of witnesses—those who have seen God's goodness and testify to His sufficiency firsthand.

This Advent season, let us run with endurance the race God has for us, casting off every sin that ensnares and joyfully pressing on to a greater knowledge of Him. Let us praise Jesus for His sacrifice on the cross and triumph over the grave. Let us examine our hearts for entangling sin, and may we trust in the greater joy of following God. Let us worship the only One who brings us to life everlasting. He is our delight and our King, the Victor who was joyful in life and death.

## LET US WORSHIP

THE ONLY ONE WHO BRINGS US TO LIFE EVERLASTING.

*Why did Jesus endure suffering with joy?*

*How does the suffering of Jesus encourage you to cast off your sin?*

*Read James 1:2-12. Why can we have joy in our suffering today?*

**WE REST SECURE
IN CHRIST.**

WEEK THREE / DAY SIX

# Joy Will Overtake Them

*Read Isaiah 35, Revelation 19:1-5*

Imagine a joy so powerful it overwhelms people and places like an invading army. Typically, we may think a superior army creates gloom and disaster. But the advances of biblical joy cause the "conquered" to celebrate, and the earth gives glory to the Victor. There is no other option but to rejoice, and all do so willingly. Scripture foreshadows this type of joy, which the saving work of God's Anointed One accomplished.

The Old Testament prophet Isaiah spoke of such elation in chapter 35 of his book. In verse 4, Isaiah preached God would come with vengeance to judge and end spiritual evil. The world's wicked would tremble at His arrival. At the same time, the faithful would find safety. In the end, God, the commander of heaven's army, would save His people. Isaiah called those saved "the ransomed" (Isaiah 35:10). "Ransomed" means God freed His people from captivity to spiritual evil and paid for their crimes. The Lord bought them, so they could live for Him and experience the joy of His presence.

Isaiah depicted the joy of the commander's salvation through the end of the covenant curse. God first pronounced this curse in Genesis 3. Adam's and Eve's disobedience plagued the earth. Lush gardens turned to dry deserts, and arable soil became rocky ground. Throughout redemptive history, sin spread and infected the hearts of all people. But, because of the Lord's victory, the wilderness and desert would transform back into fruitful places. The weak and disabled, who once were paralyzed in their grief, would jump and sing. Waters would burst from the ground, providing refreshment for the weary and nourishing the land. Finally, a highway to the kingdom of God would emerge. This path provided a safe passage for those who were righteous. These travelers were "the ransomed" we discussed earlier. God, as Victor, cleansed them from sin and placed them on the highway. He led them to His kingdom, so even if they stumbled along the way, they would not fall. They would return to the Lord's presence singing with triumphant joy.

Isaiah's prophecy was fulfilled in Jesus Christ. He was the Anointed One, sent from heaven to lead God's army. The Father gave the eternal Son a mission to save His people from bondage to sin and preserve them for Himself. Jesus accomplished this task through His life, death, and resurrection. He ministered to those who knew their deep need for a Savior. He demonstrated His power over the curse of sin by healing people from disease and raising them from the dead. Jesus declared He was the fountain of living water (John 7:37-38), who came to quench desperate people's thirst. He said He was the path to the Father (John 14:6). When He died on the cross, Jesus ended the curse. When He rose from the grave, He defeated spiritual evil and broke its hold on us. Those of us who place our faith in Jesus become "the ransomed." We are the conquered who freely celebrate Christ's victory. As we walk down Jesus's path to His kingdom, we experience the satisfaction of God's presence through His indwelling Spirit.

However, we still live in a fallen world, so we may not always experience joy overtaking us like the power of a conquering army. At times, we may even find it difficult to feel an ounce of joy when problems accumulate. How do we continue to imagine the joy that awaits us in heaven? We can meditate on Revelation 19:1-5. These verses give us a picture of the rejoicing that will take place in eternity. When Jesus returns to completely defeat His enemies and the threats against us, we all will join together and cry out His praises. We will sing, "Hallelujah! Salvation, glory, and power belong to our God, because His judgments are true and righteous" (Revelation 19:1-2). All of the earth will give witness to Jesus's glory because at His second coming, His joy will overtake us. Until that day comes, let us be confident that though we may stumble, we will not fall from the path of joy, for we rest secure in Christ.

## AT HIS SECOND COMING,

JOY WILL OVERTAKE US.

*What do today's passages reveal about God's character?*

*How does the future promise of triumphant joy affect you?*

*Read Luke 10:21. In what did Jesus rejoice? How can you mirror this joy daily in your own life?*

# WEEK THREE REFLECTION
REVIEW ALL PASSAGES FROM THE WEEK

*Summarize the main points from this week's Scripture readings.*

*What did you observe from this week's passages about God and His character?*

*What do this week's passages reveal about the condition of mankind and yourself?*

*How do these passages point to the gospel?*

*How should you respond to these passages? What specific action steps can you take this week to apply them in your life?*

*Write a prayer in response to your study of God's Word. Adore God for who He is, confess sins He revealed in your own life, ask Him to empower you to walk in obedience, and pray for anyone who comes to mind as you study.*

WEEK FOUR / DAY ONE

# CANDLE LIGHTING DAY

# love

*On the fourth Sunday of Advent, a candle is lit to symbolize love. We all crave the depth and meaning found in being truly loved. We search for it in many things, but only One can love us in the way we were purposefully and intentionally created to be loved.*

*Read John 3:16, Romans 5:8, 1 John 4*

---

Love originates in God Himself. He created the world as an overflow of His love, and He created mankind to live and dwell with them. Though mankind rebelled and rejected God, His love remained steadfast. His love was sheerly dependent on His faithful character. Sin separates us from God, but in love, God offers salvation through His Son to restore our relationship with Him. God so loved us that He made His love visible to us through the incarnation of His Son, Jesus Christ, and He made His love manifest among us through His life, death, and resurrection.

The Advent season leads us to marvel at the matchless love of Christ. No one can ever love us the way that God can, and there is no greater display of love than God sending His Son to save us from our sins. May our hearts rest secure in His sacrificial and unconditional love, and may we be compelled to share His love with the world.

## PRAYER

*Heavenly Father,*

*What sacrificial love You have shown us through the gift of Your Son, Jesus Christ! You made a promise from the very beginning to bring redemption, and we praise You, Lord, for being a promise keeper. We praise You for Your faithfulness. We praise You for Your steadfast love that has carried through the ages.*

*From being enthroned in the heavenly realms to an infant cradled in a feeding trough, we thank You, Lord, for humbling Yourself to become like us. You came near to us so that we could draw near to You. Perfection was necessary to bring us close to You, but we know, because of our sin, we could never meet that standard. So, Father, You sent Your beloved Son to live a perfect life and die a perfect death so that He could take on our sin and give us His righteousness. There is no greater love than a man who lays down his life for his friends, and You have shown us this love. We are undeserving of such a gift! We praise You for loving us in such a way.*

*We pray, Lord, that You would bring us to a sobering recognition of the gift You have given us through salvation in Jesus Christ. Through repentance and faith in Him, You have given us Your love for eternity. We pray Your love would change us and shape us into the likeness of Jesus Christ. We pray it would humble us and cultivate kindness and generosity toward others. Lord, help us to think of tangible ways to show Your love to others this season.*

*We pray You would continue to fill our hearts and minds with the truth of Your astounding love for us, and may it bring purpose and intention to this holiday season.*

*In Jesus's name we pray, Amen.*

WEEK FOUR
MEMORY VERSE

God's love was revealed among us in this way: God sent his one and only Son into the world so that we might live through him.

**1 JOHN 4:9**

**HE SEALS US WITH THE HOLY SPIRIT.**

WEEK FOUR / DAY TWO

# For God So Loved the World

*Read Ephesians 1:3-6*

Before the world was made, the Trinitarian God existed in a perfect relationship. This means that God the Father, God the Son, and God the Spirit dwelled together, united by love and holiness. The love shared among the Trinity is beyond what we can fathom, and God wanted to share it. He chose to create a world to display the wonders of His love with the expansive ocean, the shining stars, animals of every kind, trees bursting with fruit, and all the beauty of the earth. But His most magnificent creation came in the form of mankind. God created us in love to reflect Him and know Him. He made us in His image and distinct from every other living thing. He placed the first of mankind, Adam and Eve, in His beautiful garden called Eden. There He gave them everything they could ever need, and He delighted in being with them.

Adam and Eve lived in harmonious bliss with God. Until one day, Satan came to Eve as a serpent in the garden and claimed that God was withholding from them. Even with all God had given Adam and Eve, her eyes began to wander. The serpent enticed her by saying if they ate of the one tree from which God forbade them to eat, the Tree of Knowledge of Good and Evil, they would be just like God. They succumbed to the lie of a deceptive serpent and disobeyed their trustworthy God by eating from the tree. Their actions were tragic, but their hearts revealed a greater tragedy—a rejection of God's perfect love. As a response, their eyes were opened to sin, and they were afraid. By disregarding God, they broke their relationship with Him, and God cast them out of His presence.

Though sin cast humanity out of God's presence, it never cast them out of His heart. Out of His great love for His creation, He had a plan of redemption all along. Ephesians 1 affirms God's heart for His people in that He chose us to be adopted as sons through Jesus Christ before the foundation of the world. God the Father sent Jesus to take on the form of a human to be fully like us, to live righteously, and to die sacrificially in order to rescue us from our sins. John 3:16 affirms the reasoning for such a grand display of love: "For God loved the world in this way: He gave His one and only Son, so that everyone who believes in Him will not perish but have eternal life." He paid the ultimate price for our affections—His Son's life. But God did not display this unending love for us at our best. His love is steadfast and remains, despite our rebellion and sin. His love is consistent with His holy nature, and He proves this to us "in that while we were yet sinners, Christ died for us" (Romans 5:8). He is the only One capable of loving us this way. He is the only One who can know the depth of our flaws in full detail and still look on us with joy and delight. Love is displayed best as God expresses it. He is not only the author of love—He is love. His very being is the essence of love (1 John 4:16).

The story of Christmas is a story of love—that God made a way for us to restore a relationship with Him through Jesus Christ. God's love for us is so deep, so vast, so wide that it pierces through the hearts of broken sinners and invites us through repentance into a perfect relationship with Him. It changes us from the inside out, and we will never be the same. God loves us so much that He simply cannot leave us as we are. He seals us with the Holy Spirit to daily sanctify and transform us into the likeness of Christ so that when Christ returns, we will stand in Christ's righteousness and experience the love of God in full. As we celebrate the birth of Jesus Christ, may we meditate on the astounding reality that God loved us so much that He would stop at nothing to rescue and restore our relationship with Him. May the truth of this season bring fresh eyes to God's love for us, and may it tune our hearts to praise His great name!

> **HE WOULD STOP AT NOTHING** TO RESCUE AND RESTORE OUR RELATIONSHIP WITH HIM.

*How does the creation story speak to God's love for us?*

*How does the gospel showcase the love of God? How does it shape your understanding of God?*

*In what ways should God's love shape our lives? How should it shape our relationships?*

**THE GOSPEL MEETS OUR ACHE FOR LOVE.**

WEEK FOUR / DAY THREE

# A Story of Love

*Read Hosea 11:1-4, Matthew 2:13-15*

When Christmas draws near, many of us long to gather with loved ones. Commercials and advertisements paint a picture of warm meals, cozy conversations around the fire, and opening gifts around the Christmas tree with those we hold dear. Movies tell the tales of Christmas love and the sparks that follow. The perfect Christmas experience seems to require being surrounded by family and friends. And for some of us, we may hold sweet traditions and make pleasant memories with those people. But for others, we may mourn the loss of someone who will not be with us this year. We may remember drama and hardship from the previous year. We may even fight the ache of wishing our relationships were not so broken. Not all of us will experience the Christmas we see plastered before our eyes. If we find ourselves alone, we may wish for anyone to make us feel known and loved. Though we may not experience the beauty of being surrounded by loved ones in the way we desire, the true joy of Christmas is that God makes a way in His great love to invite us into a perfect relationship with Him.

God made a plan to be with His people before the beginning of time. Though God's relationship with His people took many twists and turns through each generation, we find that it was love that kept Him close. It was His love that sustained His commitment to His people. Hosea 11 illustrates God's persevering love for His children—a love so strong that it continued despite rebellion and its consequences. Hosea 11 uses the imagery of a father's love for his rebellious son, Israel. In the Old Testament, God made a promise to Abraham that He would grow his family and make it into a great nation by which He would bless all the families on the earth. This family later became Israel and was God's chosen nation, one to be his treasured possession (Deuteronomy 7:6).

The Israelites eventually found themselves in oppressive slavery in Egypt, and God enlisted Moses to lead a charge to set them free, leading them to the Promised Land. Once rescued, God provided everything they could ever need. Moses led them to Mt. Sinai, where God made a covenant with them that they would be God's people, and God would be their God. His grace protected them and sustained them as they journeyed through the wilderness. His love brought them through the Red Sea and all the way into the Promised Land of Canaan. Even with all He had done, Israel began to stray. They began to rebel and worship other gods. God was faithful, but Israel was not. Though Israel's rejection of God eventually brought on their own punishment, God never forgot them. Through the very lineage of the people of Israel, rescued from Egypt, God determined the promised Messiah would be born. God delivered His people from Egypt, and He promised to bring full deliverance through His Son, Jesus Christ.

When the time came for the promised Messiah, Jesus Christ, to be born hundreds of years later, the news reached King Herod, but he would have no one claiming to be king to contend for his throne. He set out to find this proclaimed Messiah for himself by ordering that all male children under the age of two in Bethlehem be killed. With the newborn Son of God as his target, God had other plans and appeared to Joseph in a dream, telling him to get up and take the child and his mother to Egypt until God told him it was safe to leave. So Mary and Joseph went to Egypt. It seems at this time that history is repeating itself as this family headed toward Egypt for refuge.

Matthew draws our attention to the significance of this journey by referencing the Old Testament passage of Hosea: "So he got up, took the child and his mother during the night, and escaped to Egypt. He stayed there until Herod's death, so that what was spoken by the Lord through the prophet might be fulfilled: Out of Egypt I called my Son (Matthew 2:14-15). Matthew uses this reference to identify Jesus as the fulfillment of bringing God's people out of Egypt and His loving plan of redemption for them. Jesus traveled to and from Egypt (Matthew 2:14-15, 19-21). He passed through the waters to be affirmed as God's beloved Son (Matthew 3:16-17). He went into the wilderness where He was tempted by Satan and yet did not sin (Matthew 4:1-11). Jesus followed the same path as Israel, but He remained righteous and faithful in every way that Israel failed. Jesus answered the call to live a righteous life and bear the wrath and judgment of God that Israel deserved.

Today, we find ourselves responding in ways that Israel responded. God is our Creator, giving us life and all that we need. Our response should be only heart-filled worship and awe of who He is and what He has done. But we too try to go our own way. We try to find love and care in other things. Yet, even so, God does not forget us. In love, He is patient and ready to forgive. His redemptive plan remains to restore His relationship with His children. It is love that moved the Father to send His one and only beloved Son to redeem us from our sin. It is love that moved the Son to set aside His heavenly glory so that He could give His life to save us.

No matter what relationships look like for us this Christmas season, the gospel opens the door for us to belong in the way God intended. Even though we experience loneliness, pain, and disappointment, God does not leave us to ourselves. The love we so deeply desire can be found in Christ. Through faith and repentance in Him, we experience the compassionate and sacrificial love that changes us from the inside out. The gospel meets our ache for love in that through salvation in Jesus Christ, we have a loving relationship with God, and nothing can separate us from His love that is sheerly dependent on God's holy and perfect nature. There is no story of love like God's love for His people. May we praise God for the belonging we find in Jesus Christ this season and all year round.

*How does God's relationship with Israel testify to His character?*

*How does God's compassionate love for His people reveal a different kind of love than what we might experience in the world?*

*When have you felt God's great love for you in the struggles, disappointment, and pain of this life?*

## HIS GIFT WAS THE GREATEST DISPLAY OF LOVE.

WEEK FOUR / DAY FOUR

# The Perfect Gift

*Read Galatians 4:4-7*

The holidays roll around, and many of us find ourselves searching for the perfect gifts. Gift giving is a way we show appreciation to those we love most. The desire to give is a good thing and a way that we image God. He is the perfect giver, and we get to reflect Him in our generosity toward others. But, in the middle of our gift buying efforts, there is something of insurmountable value for us to remember. The central message of Christmas is that the perfect giver loved us so much that He has given us the perfect gift—Jesus Christ.

In Luke 2, we read about the coming of a gift that God promised for centuries. The entrance of this gift to the world did not look like we might have imagined. It did not come with a grand entrance in a worldly sense, but the implications of this gift would surpass all wonders. Joseph and his fiance Mary were told in a dream that the Holy Spirit would come upon her and give her a child (Luke 1:35). This would be no ordinary child but the Holy One, the Son of God, the Savior of the world. We can only assume this would have been a terrifying and humbling thing to hear! But even so, Mary submitted her life in obedience to the Lord to carry this gift into the world.

The stage set for Jesus's birth is the essence of humility—hidden in a stable, cradled in a feeding trough, and a baby so small with a mission so large. He traded His crown for a swaddle. In a moment of birth, heaven and earth collided, and God the Son became an infant. Majesty entered meekly into the world. Romans 6:23 says, "For the wages of sin is death, but the gift of God is eternal life in Jesus Christ our Lord." We are a fallen humanity. Because of sin, we have become separated from our relationship with a loving and holy God—in both an earthly and eternal sense. The conjunction "but" in this verse that follows a hopeless situation reveals a God who offers us another way to Him outside of our own righteousness. "But the gift of God" is that He sent His one and only Son, Jesus Christ (John 3:16) to live a perfect life, take our place on the cross, and be raised from the dead. Jesus was sent to pay the penalty for our sin, and He was the only One who could do it.

The birth of Jesus Christ was the manifestation of God's great and glorious plan of redemption. He spoke through the prophets about the appointed time of His birth, and God's people had been anxiously waiting. Can you imagine the expectation? We see the promise of Jesus woven throughout the Old Testament. It carries through generations of families, rulers and kings, and the rise and fall of many nations. God held fast to His plan and continually reminded His people of what was to come. He knew His matchless and marvelous gift would be worth it all.

Can you comprehend how much God loves and cares for His people to go to such an extent to gift us with Jesus? It is unfathomable! God knew what His people needed, and He gave it to them. God is the perfect giver, and He will always give perfectly. The gift of Jesus Christ is living proof of this truth. Romans 8:32 says, "He did not even spare his own Son but offered him up for us all. How will he not also with him grant us everything?" Should we ever doubt if God has given us all that we need, may we look back to the birth of Jesus Christ, not only a gift enjoyed by those present at the time but a gift to be enjoyed by all who believe in Him as Lord and Savior. He would hang in shame so that we might stand with honor in His presence. He would be covered in blood so that we might be clothed in His righteousness. He would bear thorns so that we might wear His crown.

The truth of Jesus should be the gift we give most generously this Christmas season. We have an opportunity each December to draw our hearts and attention beyond the gifts. We have the chance to share that though these gifts are such a small display of love, God generously gives much more! His gift was the greatest display of love for us by gifting us with His Son. We can be intentional in this season of giving, marveling most at God's gift of love through Jesus Christ. May it draw our hearts beyond what lies under the tree so we can focus on what lay in the manger and the lasting joy that gift would bring to all who would receive it.

> **THE TRUTH OF JESUS**
> SHOULD BE THE GIFT WE GIVE MOST GENEROUSLY THIS CHRISTMAS SEASON.

*Salvation in Jesus Christ is an undeserved gift. How does such a gift speak to God's love for us?*

*In what ways are you prone to doubt God's love for you? How does the gift of salvation through Jesus Christ challenge those doubts?*

*What are a few practical ways you can share the love of God through the good news of the gospel this season?*

# GOD IS LOVE.

WEEK FOUR / DAY FIVE

# The Great Sacrifice

*Read 1 John 4:7-12*

A new mother forfeits hours of sleep to feed and nourish her baby. A friend relinquishes pride to apologize after hurting the feelings of someone they love. A father gives his days to long work hours to provide financially for his family. A wife sets aside her preferences to serve and care for her husband. These examples confirm that there is something about loving someone that encourages us to lay down our needs for their needs. In order to give up our own interests for the sake of another, there has to be a good enough reason. Great sacrifice is born out of love.

But even our greatest sacrifices cannot compare with the sacrifice God made to draw us near to Him in love. "God is love" (1 John 4:8). He is the origin of all that there is to know about what it means to love, and He is the necessary foundation for everything else that we believe about love. He is the source from which all love flows and the standard by which love is measured. He is the beginning and the end of love. Apart from Him, we cannot truly know the depth of what love is.

God displayed the ultimate act of love by sending His one and only Son to pay the penalty for our sin. Anyone who sins is deserving of God's wrath, and because all have sinned, all deserve that wrath (Romans 3:23). This is not a question. Romans 1:18 tells us that the wrath of God will be revealed against all ungodliness and unrighteousness, and His wrath must be satisfied. God's wrath will assuredly come, and for the unrighteous, that means death in an earthly sense but death in a spiritual sense as well. It means separation from God and the blessings of His eternal kingdom and instead experiencing eternal suffering and punishment. In order to have a relationship with God, a sacrifice for our sins must be made. The only way for God's wrath to be appeased is one of two ways: our death or Christ's death in our place. Because of God's matchless love for us, He sent His only Son, Jesus Christ, to take our place on the cross in order to satisfy His wrath.

Jesus was beaten, mocked, and scorned. He was weak and tired from carrying the weight of His own cross. His ribs were broken, and His body must have been covered with open wounds from lashing. He was then hung in gruesome agony with nails driven into His hands and feet and a crown of thorns pressed around His head. Blood would have covered His body. But the great and unimaginable pain endured on the cross was small compared to the wrath of God that bore down on Him for the sins of humanity. Jesus was wounded and killed for us. He gave up His life to purchase ours. Without His death, we would remain separated from God by our sin, and we would await the eternal punishment we deserve. There is not anything or anyone who could have saved us from our sins but Jesus.

Though Jesus died on the cross, we know He did not stay dead. Just as His crucifixion was necessary to save us, so was His resurrection. Three days after Jesus died, He was resurrected. The tomb where He was buried no longer held His earthly body, but He was raised to life and returned to His heavenly glory where He is seated at the right hand of the Father. Jesus's death paid the penalty for our sin so that we would no longer have to bear the wrath of God. His resurrection raises us to walk in His righteousness so we can have a relationship with God. His resurrection clothes us with His righteousness so that we have the privilege to enjoy a loving relationship with the Father. Through salvation in Jesus, God looks on us as He looks on Christ, with an intimate and familial love, a love for which Jesus's death and resurrection were necessary to be made complete.

When we come to the knowledge of such a love, we begin to live in light of Jesus's sacrifice, and the love of God is continually perfected within us. We grow compelled to display His love to a watching world—love that reflects patience, humility, selflessness, and joy. Love is the bond of unity for our relationship with God and our relationship with others. When we love as God created us to love, we love with purpose and truth. We love in a way that reflects and points to Christ. Christ-like love is not self-seeking. It does not look to only take and never give. It is not only offered to those who are deserving. It is not partial. It is not transactional. We reflect the love of Christ when we consider the interests of others over our own, when we are generous with compassion, and when we offer it freely with no expectation in return.

The urge to sacrifice our lives for those we love is a reflection of the gospel. Jesus Christ died a sacrificial death to bring us abundant and eternal life. We are provided small opportunities every single day to lay down our preferences and our needs for the purpose of serving and caring for others. By taking advantage of those opportunities, we reflect the love of our Savior. As we read about the life, death, and resurrection of Jesus Christ, may we be sobered by God's matchless love for us. May it fill us up, and may it overflow into the lives of those around us. May we love selflessly and sacrificially. And may we tune our hearts in praise to God who made us for Himself and stopped at nothing to restore and secure our relationship with Him for all eternity.

*What is your understanding of God's wrath? According to God's Word, who is deserving of God's wrath?*

*Why was Jesus's life, death, and resurrection necessary to appease God's wrath on our behalf?*

*How is your understanding of God's love shaped by His sacrifice of sending His Son to redeem us from our sin?*

## HE WILL LOOK AT US WITH PURE DELIGHT AND PLEASURE!

WEEK FOUR / DAY SIX

# The Culmination of God's Love

*Read Zephaniah 3:14-17*

The feelings that follow our anticipation of something can change depending on how its arrival will affect us. Consider the differing reactions you might incite in a child when you say, "Yay! Dad is home!" or "You just wait until your dad gets home." The expectation for one is joy, and the other is fear. A child will anticipate a dad's arrival with excitement and relief, knowing it will bring joy to his or her life, but that child will wait in dread and fear, knowing it will bring punishment and judgment. An important question to consider as we study our Lord Jesus Christ's coming arrival during this Advent season is whether we anticipate His coming arrival with joy or fear.

During the time of the prophet Zephaniah, the entire nation of Israel feared the Lord's coming. The Israelites seemed to have followed in the same ways of our first parents, Adam and Eve. God created Adam and Eve and placed them in the bountiful garden of Eden, where God cared for them and dwelled with them. But instead of gratitude and worship, they rebelled against God and sinned. So, God cast them out of the garden and removed them from His presence. Adam and Eve's offspring continued in rebellion to the extent of being only evil all the time (Genesis 6:5), so God brought another form of exile by flooding the earth. After the flood, the nation of Israel was formed through Abraham, Isaac, and Jacob, but because of their sin, Israel fell into the hands of the Egyptians and suffered enslavement for 400 years.

The Lord eventually rescued Israel out of Egypt, with Moses leading the charge. God led them to the Promised Land, where they began to establish themselves. At the height of their glory, during the reign of King David, the nation became rebellious again and turned to worship false gods and bow down to idols. Therefore, God sent the prophets to counsel them with His words and warn them of what would come if they continued in rebellion. The Israelites disregarded these warnings and continued in their ways. So God kept His promise of judgment, and the Babylonians conquered their city and held them in exile for 70 years. Just as Adam and Eve were cast out of the garden of Eden, Israel was exiled and cast out of the Promised Land.

The Israelites sought their fulfillment in things apart from the Lord, leading them to turn away from God, who so loved them, and become enslaved to their sin. Our hearts are inclined to do the same. We reject God and seek other things in hopes that they will fill us up and make our lives feel meaningful. But the consequences leave us in our own form of spiritual exile. Sin separates us from God, and when we indulge in sin, we forfeit our relationship with Him. In the comfort and security of God's love is where all meaning and purpose for this life are found. He knows the depths of our hearts and fulfills our every need. Even when we fail Him, He will never fail us. His warnings and commands for repentance are not simply for His glory but also for our good! The best the world can offer us is temporary satisfaction, but God can offer us untouchable joy for eternity. Why would we not turn to him in repentance and faith?

The bulk of the book of Zephaniah concerns judgment and the punishment Israel brought upon themselves by continuing their sin-filled ways. God called the prophet to speak against the moral demise of Israel, so Zephaniah pleaded with Israel and warned them of the day of the Lord when they would face the consequences of their sin—the wrath of God poured out through the Babylonians who would bring destruction in their land and carry the Israelites into captivity. But the last portion of the book takes a surprising and hopeful turn. For those who heeded the warnings of the Lord—those who listened and repented of their ways—Zephaniah spoke of joy instead of judgment for them. After being humbled in exile, God would begin to restore them. In this coming restoration, God commanded Zion to sing with joy and rejoice in gladness because the Lord had removed their punishment and turned away their enemies. He would replace their fear with joy and bring restoration and redemption to their land. The Israelites bore the consequences of their sin, but God would not cast them out of His presence forever.

The prophecy of Zephaniah was fulfilled in part in the first coming of Jesus Christ when God initiated reconciliation by taking the form of a human and dwelling among us. God the Son was born in the flesh to liberate us from sin and deliver us from spiritual exile. Even though God's people chose rebellion, God chose restoration, and we find redemption from our sins through salvation in Jesus Christ. For all who put their hope and faith in Him, their punishment for sin and deserved wrath is removed, and they are freed to walk in a loving relationship with God.

But the final fulfillment of Zephaniah's prophecy will happen at the second advent of the Lord. When Jesus returns in His glory, He will destroy Satan and eradicate sin once and for all. He will gather His people from all over the earth and unite them under the banner of His name. He will restore His bounty and look on His people with love and delight. As Christians, our response to the Lord's coming should be an eager and joyful expectation.

On that day, we will be face to face with our Savior, and our hearts will overflow with praise. We will sing and dance and be filled with joy! There will be no more sin, no more sorrow, no more trials, no more temptation, and no more death! We will be perfected in every way and crowned with the complete righteousness of Christ. Our every need will be met, and our every hope will be fulfilled. We will see the crescendo of our salvation. God will rejoice over us and quiet us in His love. He will look at us with pure delight and pleasure! We will bask in the radiance of His glory, knowing His love in a way we have never known before. We will experience in full the breadth and depth, height and length, and everlasting strength of God's astounding love for us. We will be His people, and He will be our God forevermore.

*When you think of the Lord's return, do you anticipate His coming arrival with joy or fear? What determines those emotions for you?*

*God brings restoration through repentance and faith. How have you experienced God's restorative ways?*

*God so loves us that He does not partially fulfill His promises. How does the news of the second coming of Christ bring God's love for you full circle?*

# Christ Candle

*The Christ candle is traditionally a long, white candle placed in the middle of an advent wreath. Lit on Christmas Eve, it represents the life of Christ.*

*Read Luke 2, Isaiah 9:6*

---

This Christmas Eve, we celebrate the coming of Jesus. Our long-awaited Savior has arrived! Born to poor, humble parents, Jesus came as a baby to embody the mystery of salvation. Though He is King of kings and Lord of lords, He was born in a dirty stable meant for animals, a lowly manger for His head. He entered the world in the darkness of night to triumph over our eternal darkness and bring us light.

As we light this candle today, we remember the faultless life of our Savior. The humble baby, the perfect boy, the meek man, the Suffering Servant, and the King of kings. The One who knelt to wash the feet of His friends and healed the untouchables cast out from the rest of society, the teacher who made much of God and joyfully taught His commands, the Lamb led willingly to the slaughter, the Son who obeyed the Father to a gruesome death on a nail-pierced cross, and the Victor who trumped sin and death forever.

Every week in Advent, we have lit candles to meditate on the reason for our hope, peace, joy, and love. Today, as we light the Christ candle, we rejoice as we celebrate that Christ has come! We worship because Jesus is our hope in all seasons; He has overcome the world. We praise God because Jesus is our peace, the only way we as sinners can have peace with a holy God. He is our joy, saving us from eternal damnation and bringing us into His holy kingdom as His heirs. And oh, how He loves us. He is love incarnate, the long-awaited promise finally fulfilled.

This King now lives interceding for us, and He will one day come again to rule over all. Just as Jesus came that unexpected night, He is coming again. Let us prepare Him room.

### PRAYER

*Oh Lord, How majestic is Your name in all the earth! The heavens declare Your glory, and so do we. You are the One we hoped for, Jesus, the long-awaited answer to our suffering and pain. You are the promise fulfilled, the reason we can have hope, peace, joy, and love. You are the fulfillment of every prophecy, every covenant, every longing, every hope. You have come, loving us when we were unlovable and forgiving us our unbearable load of sin. You have called us Your sons and daughters. Thank You. Your name, Jesus, is the sweetest name we know.*

*Though we can so often grow numb to Your sacrifice, we look to You with fresh eyes today. You have always been the answer. Your life has set us free from our bondage. Your death saved us from sin. Your resurrection promises us new life.*

*Even as we praise You for what You have done, we remember that You are coming again. Take residence in our hearts and change us so that we can better honor Your name. Be King over our hearts and our lives. Thank You for coming to save us. We love You, Lord. We are Yours.*

*Amen.*

# WEEK FOUR REFLECTION
REVIEW ALL PASSAGES FROM THE WEEK

*Summarize the main points from this week's Scripture readings.*

*What did you observe from this week's passages about God and His character?*

*What do this week's passages reveal about the condition of mankind and yourself?*

*How do these passages point to the gospel?*

*How should you respond to these passages? What specific action steps can you take this week to apply them in your life?*

*Write a prayer in response to your study of God's Word. Adore God for who He is, confess sins He revealed in your own life, ask Him to empower you to walk in obedience, and pray for anyone who comes to mind as you study.*

# WHAT IS THE GOSPEL?

*Thank you for reading and enjoying this study with us! We are abundantly grateful for the Word of God, the instruction we glean from it, and the ever-growing understanding it provides for us of God's character. We are also thankful that Scripture continually points to one thing in innumerable ways: the gospel.*

We remember our brokenness when we read about the fall of Adam and Eve in the garden of Eden (Genesis 3), where sin entered into a perfect world and maimed it. We remember the necessity that something innocent must die to pay for our sin when we read about the atoning sacrifices in the Old Testament. We read that we have all sinned and fallen short of the glory of God (Romans 3:23) and that the penalty for our brokenness, the wages of our sin, is death (Romans 6:23). We all need grace and mercy, but most importantly, we all need a Savior.

We consider the goodness of God when we realize that He did not plan to leave us in this dire state. We see His promise to buy us back from the clutches of sin and death in Genesis 3:15. And we see that promise accomplished with Jesus Christ on the cross. Jesus Christ knew no sin yet became sin so that we might become righteous through His sacrifice (2 Corinthians 5:21). Jesus was tempted in every way that we are and lived sinlessly. He was reviled yet still yielded Himself for our sake, that we may have life abundant in Him. Jesus lived the perfect life that we could not live and died the death that we deserved.

The gospel is profound yet simple. There are many mysteries in it that we will never understand this side of heaven, but there is still overwhelming weight to its implications in this life. The gospel tells of our sinfulness and God's goodness and a gracious gift that compels a response. We are saved by grace through faith, which means that we rest with faith in the grace that Jesus Christ displayed on the cross (Ephesians 2:8-9). We cannot save ourselves from our brokenness or do any amount of good works to merit God's favor. Still, we can have faith that what Jesus accomplished in His death, burial, and resurrection was more than enough for our salvation and our eternal delight. When we accept God, we are commanded to die to ourselves and our sinful desires and live a life worthy of the calling we have received (Ephesians 4:1). The gospel compels us to be sanctified, and in so doing, we are conformed to the likeness of Christ Himself. This is hope. This is redemption. This is the gospel.

SCRIPTURES TO REFERENCE:

| | |
|---|---|
| GENESIS 3:15 | *I will put hostility between you and the woman, and between your offspring and her offspring. He will strike your head, and you will strike his heel.* |
| ROMANS 3:23 | *For all have sinned and fall short of the glory of God.* |
| ROMANS 6:23 | *For the wages of sin is death, but the gift of God is eternal life in Christ Jesus our Lord.* |
| 2 CORINTHIANS 5:21 | *He made the one who did not know sin to be sin for us, so that in him we might become the righteousness of God.* |
| EPHESIANS 2:8-9 | *For you are saved by grace through faith, and this is not from yourselves; it is God's gift—not from works, so that no one can boast.* |
| EPHESIANS 4:1-3 | *Therefore I, the prisoner in the Lord, urge you to walk worthy of the calling you have received, with all humility and gentleness, with patience, bearing with one another in love, making every effort to keep the unity of the Spirit through the bond of peace.* |

*Thank you for studying
God's Word with us!*

**CONNECT WITH US**
@thedailygraceco
@dailygracepodcast

**CONTACT US**
info@thedailygraceco.com

**SHARE**
#thedailygraceco

**VISIT US ONLINE**
thedailygraceco.com

**MORE DAILY GRACE**
The Daily Grace App
Daily Grace Podcast